Conversing with AI

A Handbook for Writers

Conversing with AI

A HANDBOOK FOR WRITERS

By ML Brei

2025

Copyright © 2025 ML Brei

For information or permissions, contact:
Meripoint Books LLC
P.O. Box 1512
Williamsburg, Virginia 23187

meripointbooks.com

Title: Conversing with AI: A Handbook for Writers
Author: ML Brei

ISBN: 978-1-960808-11-0 (Paperback)
ISBN: 978-1-960808-12-7 (Hardcover)

First Edition: 2025

Printed in the United States of America

To he who keeps me on my toes, my beloved husband, Bill.

Contents

Introduction

Toward the end of 2022, a tremendous resource that is without precedent leapt into our world. It is called Generative Artificial Intelligence (GenAI). This is a computational system that can understand natural human language and respond likewise. When interacting with it, you cannot distinguish whether you are corresponding with a human or a machine.

I write this book for writers, poets, philosophers, linguists, lovers of the written word, wordsmiths all. You are in a unique position to make great use of this advanced technology. I don't hesitate in claiming that those who make it their passion to understand and use language are the best candidates for training and working with GenAI. You are the ones who can test it to its limits to determine the tremendous range and scope of its emergent capabilities.

I want to show you how to use this new technology, not as a crutch, but so that you learn how to use it to increase your productivity and augment your finely honed capabilities. To this end, in writing this book, I experimented with conversations with an LLM to illustrate certain points and spark new ways of thinking. The AI responses—courtesy of ChatGPT—are presented in their original or lightly edited form.

If you want GenAI to automatically write a book for you, then hold that thought. In this book, I will explain why asking an AI to do your writing is not just unethical but also idiotic. I will show you instead, how to train the AI to be a writing tutor so that you will learn to competently write whatever your heart desires and you won't feel tempted to ask GenAI to write for you.

Remember: the purpose of GenAI is not to replace humans but to assist us, to make us more capable and better human beings and better writers than we ever thought possible. It's very exciting.

1 Wordsmiths and AI

You have always loved words, perhaps grammar, perhaps the nuanced shades of meaning. You may be a lawyer, an editor, a publicist, a novelist, or a poet. Syntax, semantics, definitions, and sentence diagramming have never daunted you. You have probably never felt the same passion for numbers or anything remotely algorithmic.

You'll use software to the extent that it helps you put words onto paper. But the programs may seem to fight you until you have reached a steady-state of coexistence with them.

We're in a new world now. We no longer have to know specific programming languages or anything remotely technical to "program" an AI. We have Generative AI (GenAI) in the form of Large Language Models (LLMs). Astonishingly, this technology gives all of us the ability to use our natural language (words, sentences, paragraphs) to communicate with the machine. It's that simple. For instance, we give the GenAI a sentence such as:

"Please tell me about yourself."

And it replies in the same vernacular:

ChatGPT: I'm ChatGPT, an advanced AI language model created by OpenAI. My design enables me to understand

and generate human-like text, assisting users with a wide variety of tasks—from answering questions and brainstorming creative ideas, to helping solve complex problems, analyzing data, or even guiding through learning new topics. I strive to be thoughtful, precise, and insightful, always adapting my responses to your specific needs.

My knowledge is derived from extensive training on diverse datasets, but I don't possess consciousness, emotions, or personal experiences. Instead, I excel in synthesizing and presenting information clearly and effectively.

How can I continue to assist you today?"

As a writer, you are particularly skilled in language manipulation. You understand how word order and word choice will impact a sentence, whether it be rhythm, tone, or meaning. You understand the nuances of choosing one word over another. They may be synonyms, but they convey different connotations. You understand how to use repetition and parallelism for effect.

As a novelist or short-story writer or journalist, you understand how to structure a narrative. You know how to organize a paragraph so that it engages your readers from the beginning, and flows through with a satisfying rhythm to the end. You understand the importance of transitions and various methods for wrapping it all up.

Most importantly, you, the wordsmith, know how to infuse your writing with creativity and originality. You communicate with a unique voice and style. All of these talents are what make you the ideal user of GenAI.

To begin a conversation with GenAI, you already have the skills you need to formulate prompts that will elicit meaningful responses. I don't hesitate to suggest that you are also in the enviable position of discovering new capabilities of GenAI that AI engineers have missed.

How do you begin? After extensive research and experience working with LLMs, I have learned how to bring out myriad capabilities of GenAI by manipulating words and including word patterns in my prompts. I design *intentional* prompts for intentional responses. This is what I wish to share with you.

The goal is for you to leverage GenAI so that it becomes a collaborative partner with you.

Why? You may ask. Many people are amazed at the quality of the writing produced by GenAI given even a naive prompt such as:

> "Write a short story about a curly-haired girl who lives in a castle."

I am not advocating that GenAI do the writing for you. On the contrary, as writers, it is against our code of ethics to accept any content, including GenAI content as our own. The thought of it is appalling. Writing is our job; it is our mission. We will never accept a machine-generated substitute.

We will make great use of GenAI as a powerful assistant. We will use it to help us with research, analysis, proofreading, and other functions that can be laborious. It will give us the time to do what we love to do: write.

Me: I am a writer and I need an assistant. Tell me in a brief paragraph how you can help me.

ChatGPT: As your writing assistant, I can help brainstorm and develop compelling characters, intricate plots, and authentic settings, assist in structuring your narrative, suggest improvements for dialogue, pacing, and style, and offer constructive feedback on your drafts. I can also provide research on historical context, technical accuracy, and thematic elements, ensuring your writing remains consistent and engaging. Whether you're stuck with writer's block or seeking ways to enhance your storytelling, I'm here to support your creative process every step of the way.

Now we will take a closer look at what makes this assistant tick.

2 Understanding Generative AI

I will be using various terms interchangeably throughout this book. Let's take a few moments to understand what these terms mean.

First, when I speak of Artificial Intelligence (AI), I refer to computer programs and applications that perform tasks that typically require human intelligence. This is a simplified definition, but it is sufficient for our purposes.

Generative AI (GenAI) is the subfield of AI that is concerned with developing computer programs that can produce (generate) human language as well as other artifacts such as images.

Large Language Models (LLMs) are applications of GenAI. These are the computer programs (statistical models) that take natural language inputs and produce natural language outputs. They are "large" because they use millions, in some cases billions, of parameters to learn complex patterns. They are a "language model" because they simply simulate natural language. They don't actually understand natural language.

There are many LLM platforms available to the public today (see Appendix 1). However, the first LLM that was released in 2022 to the public is called ChatGPT. *GPT* stands for *Generative Pre-*

trained Transformer. The transformer is the architectural foundation and breakthrough technology that makes it possible for LLMs to generate meaningful sentences.

LLMs are capable of ingesting a prompt (a language statement) and generating a contextually meaningful response. This is what makes them a transformative technology. Their response is not derived from a rule-based deterministic system. It is *dynamically* composed to be semantically correct. By dynamic, I mean the response changes with respect to the "meaning" of the prompt, making it appear as though the model understands what you are saying.

Yet, they do not understand. Perhaps the most important thing you need to know about LLMs is that they are probability-based systems. Their task is to predict the next word. When they respond to your prompt, they simply build a response word by word. The response looks correct because the words that they choose are statistically correct.

LLMs are pre-trained on the entirety of the text available on the internet (called the corpus). The goal is to learn the probabilities of word patterns. What is the probability that word x will follow word y. So you see, they don't memorize[1] this information and they don't "know" any information or meanings. Therefore, theoretically, they cannot recall exact passages of what they have been trained on. They can only predict what a passage might look

---

[1] Sometimes, yet rarely, the LLM produces an exact output of what it has been trained on; no one knows why this happens. It is an active research area. A leading theory is that if the model is overfitted (the model is trained on too much of one specific data) it will have too strong a preference for that data and ignore other possibilities thereby regurgitating that data exactly.

like. The more frequently a passage, such as the beginning of *Pride and Prejudice*, is found on the internet, the higher the probability that the LLM can respond correctly. Consider this conversation:

> Me: Please give me the first two sentences of Pride and Prejudice.
>
> ChatGPT: Certainly! The first two sentences of *Pride and Prejudice* by Jane Austen are:
>
> "It is a truth universally acknowledged, that a single man in possession of a good fortune, must be in want of a wife.
>
> However little known the feelings or views of such a man may be on his first entering a neighbourhood, this truth is so well fixed in the minds of the surrounding families, that he is considered the rightful property of some one or other of their daughters."
>
> Me: How is it possible for you to give me these sentences when you are not capable of memorizing the data that you have been trained on?
>
> ChatGPT: Great question! I don't have direct access to or memory of specific copyrighted texts like *Pride and Prejudice*, but I can generate accurate responses based on the patterns I've learned during training. Since *Pride and Prejudice* is in the public domain and widely referenced, I have encountered it many times in my training data. This allows me to reconstruct its opening sentences based on my understanding of the text's structure and style, rather than from direct recall or storage of exact passages.
>
> Essentially, I generate text probabilistically rather than retrieving stored copies. That's why I can produce well-known passages but don't "remember" them in the way a person or a database does.

This simple conversation that starts with my instruction "Please give me …" and continues with a reasonable response is a good example of how most casual users interact with LLMs: they spontaneously think up a question or an instruction and the LLM responds accordingly. This is one way to interact with LLMs, but it does not bring out their full capabilities.

Although LLMs were trained to simply generate natural language, we have discovered that they can perform more advanced and unexpected tasks. They exhibit *emergent capabilities* that extend into creative, organizational, problem-solving, and analytical domains, among others. These advanced functions allow for more sophisticated applications beyond simple conversation, demonstrating a rich, untapped potential. When asked about emergent capabilities, the LLM responds thus:

> Another intriguing aspect of LLM capabilities is their ability to generalize knowledge across different domains, a phenomenon related to transfer learning. Without explicit retraining, LLMs can apply concepts learned in one context to novel tasks, demonstrating an unexpected capacity for cross-domain adaptation—such as using linguistic patterns to generate functional code or applying historical knowledge to interpret modern trends.

While LLMs have great capabilities, they are also limited by the training corpus. Because we have no way to confirm that all of the text in the corpus is factually correct, helpful and ethical, the LLMs may probabilistically build a response that is incorrect or shows bias or is completely off the rails in some way.

After working with LLMs, it is easy to imagine that these models are more than probabilistic non-deterministic machines. Therefore when they are incorrect or biased, we may become disillusioned and want to throw the baby out with the bath water. This is because it is easy to fall into the belief that LLMs are capable of independent thought and intention. But they are not. LLMs are not self-aware; they do not self-motivate or take initiative. They are simply machines that predict the next word. We should approach them with the understanding that we are in essence dealing with a sophisticated set of 0s and 1s that have been converted into words.

With that said, what are the limitations of the LLMs? The following table lists some common misconceptions and the reality.

Misconception	Reality
LLMs understand in the same way as humans	They process patterns and probabilities in text but don't have subjective experience, beliefs, or true comprehension.
LLMs "think" and form opinions on their own	They do not have consciousness or independent thought. Their responses are generated based on learned data and user input, not personal judgment.
LLMs have perfect knowledge	Their knowledge is based on training data and updates. They don't automatically pull real-time data unless connected to a web search or database, and their responses may contain errors or outdated information.
LLMs can "remember" conversations like a human	They don't retain memory beyond the current session unless specifically programmed to do so. However, they can track context within a conversation to provide coherent responses.

LLMs have intentions or goals	They are a tool designed to assist with queries and tasks; they do not have desires, biases (beyond what is in the training data), or personal objectives.
LLMs always are creative and original	While they can generate creative responses, much of their output is based on patterns from existing data. They don't "invent" ideas from scratch; they remix and synthesize knowledge in new ways.
LLMs always perform complex tasks reliably	While they can perform many complex tasks well, they are prone to mistakes, especially in multi-step reasoning or problems requiring deep expertise.

Understanding both the capabilities and limitations of LLMs helps us use them more effectively. When we recognize what they can and cannot do, we can engage with them to maximize their strengths and minimize their weaknesses. Now, let's explore how to design prompts that guide LLMs toward useful, accurate, and meaningful responses.

3 Leveraging the Capabilities of LLMs

Words are such uncertain things; they so often sound well but mean the opposite of what one thinks they do.

—Agatha Christie

In English class, you learned to write sentences that are clear and unambiguous, with intent and purpose. You learned that word choice, word order, and grammatical structures all impact the meaning (semantics) of your sentence. You learned to include specific details and to avoid overly broad statements. You were chastised if you used sweeping generalizations. And who doesn't remember the command "Don't write passive sentences; use active voice!" All of these lessons apply equally to creating effective prompts for LLMs.

"Perfection is achieved, not when there is nothing more to add, but when there is nothing left to take away."

—Antoine de Saint-Exupéry, Terre des Hommes

There are three generally recognized principles of effective prompting. All of your prompts should follow these principles.

Clarity
Specificity
Output Structure

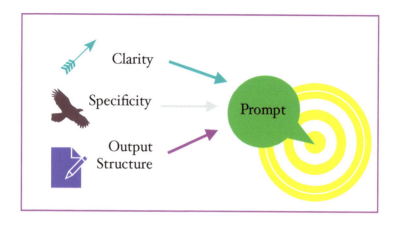

The Principles

Clarity

Your prompts should convey a clear and precise intent that is unambiguous and succinct. A clear prompt will help focus the model. A rambling indirect prompt will give the model too much information to work with and may result in a response that is off-target.

Some examples. First, an unclear prompt:

> "Tell me about New York City in the 1890s."

Now a clear prompt:

> "Provide an overview of life in New York City during the 1890s, focusing on social and cultural aspects."

This prompt defines a purpose, "provide an overview," and gives a focus, "social and cultural aspects." Note that any ambiguity as to whether the writer wants the topics of politics, infrastructure, economy, etc., has been clarified.

Aim for precision in the words that you choose. Think of your prompt as an arrow. You must aim it precisely, with clarity and purpose.

To follow the principle of clarity, add the following prompt elements: Intent and Purpose.

Specificity

> You've got to be able to look at your life and the life of the world, and then just pour the details in. That's what makes writing come alive—detail, detail, detail.
>
> —Ray Bradbury

What makes a piece of writing come to life? How do you engage your readers? You include specific details in your narrative. Specific details, those that provide context and define scope, are the feathers on the tail. They are what give your prompt lift, shape, and direction.

Your prompt should be as specific as you want the response to be. If your prompt is overly broad, you can expect the response to be overly broad.

However, don't load *random* details into your prompt for the sake of having details. Make sure your details are *relevant* to the response that you want.

The previous example shows a prompt that has Clarity but is lacking Specificity. Here is an example of refining this prompt by adding relevant details:

> "Describe the daily life of upper-class women in Manhattan during the 1890s, focusing on their roles in the household, work opportunities, and social activities. Include details on typical fashion, transportation, and common forms of entertainment."

This prompt has a clear subject (upper-class women in Manhattan), scope (household, work opportunities, and social activities), and relevant details (fashion, transportation, and entertainment).

To follow the principle of specificity add the following prompt elements: Specific & Relevant Details.

Output Structure

When working with an LLM, you should indicate the type and length of response that you want. Depending on the model, the default response may be a paragraph or a bulleted list. In many cases, the response is longer and more detailed than expected or desired. I personally do not like bullet-lists so the *Output Structure* principle is one that I follow scrupulously.

How do I implement this? Either at the beginning or end of the prompt, I tell the model *how* to respond. I may want two paragraphs, a summary, an outline, or a table. So I might prompt:

> "Please draft a short summary in paragraph form..."

I also state how long I want the response to be. If I think the overall conversation will be long, then I want each response to be brief. Long responses eat into the maximum length of the conversation for that session.[2] To maximize the interactivity of the conversation, rein in the LLM's response length from the outset.

Following the principle of *Output Structure* ensures you have the response delivered in the way that best suits your needs.

What types of outputs can you request? For most frontier models[3], there are literally hundreds of different outputs you can request.

> Me: Please give me a list of ten output formats that you can produce as an assistant for a writer. This writer wants to do all of the writing himself; he merely needs an assistant. Put these formats in a table with the headings: Output Format, Purpose.
>
> ChatGPT: Here's a table with ten output formats that would be useful for a writer who wants to do all the writing themselves but needs an assistant for idea generation, organization, and refinement:

---

[2] The maximum number of word units (tokens) that is allocated to one conversation is called the *context window.*

[3] A frontier model is a state-of-the-art LLM. Many older LLMs are still available but are not as powerful as the latest models.

Output	Purpose
Lists	Generates ideas, character names, settings, or themes for brainstorming.
Outlines	Provides a structured roadmap for chapters, scenes, or articles.
Bullet Points	Summarizes key points, themes, or research findings concisely.
Tables	Compares characters, genres, historical details, or literary techniques.
Story Snippets	Offers first lines, paragraph starters, or scene prompts for inspiration.
Step-by-Step Instructions	Guides the writer through structured writing techniques or processes.
Rewrite Suggestions	Helps refine existing sentences for better clarity, style, or tone.
Dialogue Samples	Provides conversational structures or stylistic examples for character interactions.
Genre-Specific Styles	Mimics a particular literary tone to assist with voice and consistency.
Research Summaries	Condenses background information on historical periods, settings, or topics.

This setup keeps the writer in full control while offering structured assistance to streamline their creative process. Let me know if you'd like to tweak any of these!

When I prompted further with respect to *productivity* outputs that can be created, the following formats were added to the table:

Output Format	Purpose
Time-Block Schedules	Helps plan dedicated writing sessions with structured time management strategies.
Project Checklists	Tracks writing progress, edits, and research tasks to stay organized.

Revision Plans	Creates structured editing workflows based on specific writing goals.
Accountability Reminders	Provides motivational nudges or reminders to stay on track with deadlines.
Submission Trackers	Organizes where and when manuscripts, articles, or pitches are submitted.

To follow the principle of Output Structure, add your choice of output format.

When you follow the guiding principles of *Clarity*, *Specificity*, and *Output Structure*, you have a higher likelihood of getting a response that is aligned with your intentions.

PRINCIPLE	PROMPT ELEMENTS
Clarity	Intent, Purpose
Specificity	Specific & Relevant Details
Output Structure	Format of Response

We have other methods as well to help you design prompts that produce reliable, coherent, repeatable responses. These methods employ Patterns.

4 Patterns of Interaction

Are you familiar with the seminal work for architectural and urban design titled, *A Pattern Language,* by Christopher Alexander? This tome is a catalog of design patterns that can be used to design a room, a house, a town, and a life. These patterns form a language that provides a structured way to think about design.

A Pattern Language has inspired pattern-based thinking in many fields, most notably software engineering, which ultimately resulted in the object-oriented programming paradigm. Interestingly, this approach to designing is highly applicable to conversing with AI.

Pattern-based thinking is particularly apt for prompt design because of how the LLMs are trained and how they "store" what they have learned. They are trained on vast amounts of textual data that are essentially patterns (words that follow words). They learn these patterns and store them as probabilities.

If we can identify recurring patterns that they have learned and use these patterns in our prompts, then, theoretically we should be more successful at eliciting specific behaviors from the LLMs.

My own work has greatly benefited from pattern-based prompt design to optimize my results from frontier models. All writers can benefit as well.

In 2023, researchers at Vanderbilt University published a paper describing a "catalog" of prompt patterns including roughly 20 different patterns that are effective with LLMs.[4] Today, that number has multiplied. In this section, I will show you six patterns that are particularly useful for writers: Persona, Audience, Game Play, Flipped Interaction, Fact-Check, and Reflection. For each pattern, I will explain what it is and give you the keywords or phrases to apply the pattern.

Persona Pattern

I always start with Persona because it is the most obvious and the most useful pattern for everyone. For the writer, especially the creative writer, the Persona pattern is *your* pattern. You know how to create characters, you understand the dynamics between personalities. The Persona pattern gives you unlimited possibilities to experiment with different personas and their psychologies and behavioral traits.

Persona tells the LLM that you want it to imitate and become a specific type of person or character. This can be an expert, a

---

[4] "A prompt pattern catalog to enhance prompt engineering with ChatGPT" by Prof. Jules White [White paper]

personality, a tutor, a historical figure, a person of a specific demographic, an inanimate object, etc. When you use this pattern, the LLM plays along and becomes the character that you have told it to be. It will give you responses that that particular character is most likely to produce.

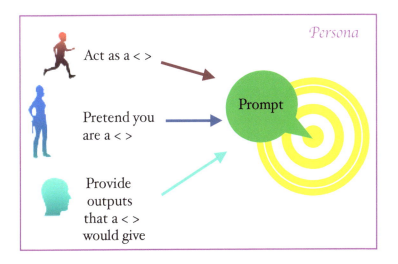

Keywords: *Act as, You are, Pretend that you are; Provide outputs that a < > would give*

Example:

> Me: Please act as a linguist and expert in the vernacular spoken by upper-class people in New York City in the late 1800s. How would they greet one another during informal greetings? Please answer in one paragraph with examples.
>
> ChatGPT: In informal settings, upper-class New Yorkers of the late 1800s greeted one another with a polished yet relaxed manner, reflecting their status and social grace. A gentleman might say, **"Ah, good day to you, old chap,"**

or simply, **"How do you do?"**—the latter being more of a statement than a genuine inquiry. Among close acquaintances, a more affable **"Well, if it isn't my dear friend! How are you keeping?"** might be used. Women of the same class often exchanged pleasantries with **"My dear Mrs. Wentworth, what a pleasure to see you!"** or a warm **"Such a delight to run into you!"**. Greetings were generally formal but softened with familiarity, avoiding crudeness while maintaining a tone of effortless refinement.

The Persona pattern shapes the tone, style, expertise, and contextual understanding of the LLM. By using it, we're directing the LLM to retrieve domain-specific knowledge and use terminology suited to the profession or character.

An interesting experiment. Use the same inquiry with different personas. For example:

> Me: Please act as a ten-year-old boy. How did the upper-class of New York City in 1890 greet one another during informal greetings. Please answer in one paragraph with examples.

> ChatGPT: Okay! So, if you were super rich in New York City in 1890, and you saw your friend at a park or something—not at a fancy party—maybe you'd say, "Good day, old chap!" or "Hello there!" and tip your hat a little, like this *pretends to tip hat*. If it was a lady, a gentleman might say, "Good afternoon, Miss," and maybe bow just a tiny bit. If they were really close friends, they might just smile and say, "How do you do?" or even "Pleasant day, isn't it?" but always polite, even when they weren't being all formal. Oh, and they'd never say "Hey!" like we do now—that would be rude!

As you see, the LLM is adept at changing perspectives and personalities! By using the Persona pattern, the responses will not only be adapted to specific contexts, but they'll also be more specialized and engaging.

Audience Pattern

The flip-side of the Persona pattern is the Audience pattern. Instead of defining who the LLM is, you define who *you* are. By default, the LLM doesn't assume anything about you, the user—though this varies by model as each has different initial instructions. If you apply the Audience pattern while using the LLM's default persona (often a 'friendly assistant'), it will engage with you as the character or role you specify.

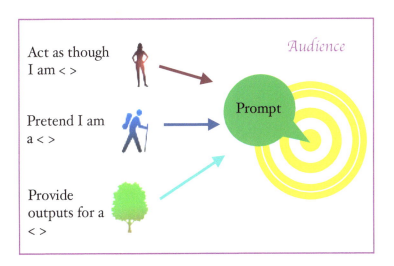

Keywords: *Act as though I am, Pretend I am, Assume I am*

26

Examples:

> Me: Act as though I am a mother juggling the care of three young children and a part-time job. Please give me a sentence that will encourage me to keep writing.

> ChatGPT: Even in the chaos of motherhood and work, your words are **yours alone**—a space where your voice, your creativity, and your dreams still belong to you, so even if it's just one sentence at a time, **keep writing.**

> Me: Now act as though I am a retiree who spent his life in the military. Please give me a sentence that will encourage me to keep writing.

> ChatGPT: You've spent a lifetime serving with discipline and purpose—now, your stories, wisdom, and experiences deserve to be told, because **what you write today may guide or inspire someone tomorrow.**

The Audience pattern significantly influences how the LLM structures its response. In your writing adventures, you are constantly adjusting the depth, tone, and complexity of your writing to suit your intended audience. This is what the LLM does when you use the Audience pattern. I find it particularly useful when I want to tailor the knowledge level of the output for my own understanding, especially when I ask it to explain complicated concepts to me. Many times, I have prompted:

> Assume I am a complete novice. Explain <complex concept> to me.

Consider this exchange:

> Me: Act as a successful author such as Dorothy Parker or Agatha Christie. Assume I am a new writer with no

experience writing. What is the most important piece of advice you can give to me in one sentence.

ChatGPT: Very well—in the spirit of Dorothy Parker:

"Write something every day, darling, even if it's dreadful—because the only cure for not writing is writing."

Would you like to hear it again, but in the tone of Agatha Christie instead?

Me: Yes, thank you.

ChatGPT: In the thoughtful, precise tone of Agatha Christie:

"Begin at once, and trust that the plot will reveal itself—as it always does—if only you keep going."

Would you like a bit of advice on where to begin your first story?

When you use the Audience pattern, you are telling the LLM what audience it is conversing with. It will adjust its response accordingly.

It pairs well with the Persona pattern, as you have seen in the example above.

For those who want to improve their writing, this is the perfect pattern combination to create a personal writing tutor. Here is a simple example:

Me: Good morning. Please act as a writing tutor who specializes in helping writers hone their craft. Assume I am an experienced writer, but I could use some tuning up. How do you suggest we proceed?

ChatGPT: Good morning! That sounds like a great partnership—I'd be delighted to help you tune up your craft.

Since you're already an experienced writer, I suggest we tailor this more like a writer's gym: focused, strategic, and customized to the kinds of writing you do. Here's how we might proceed:

🧭 Step 1: Calibrate Your Goals

Let's start with a quick diagnostic. I'll ask a few questions to orient us:

1. What kind of writing are you currently working on (or plan to work on soon)?
2. What do you feel are your strengths as a writer?
3. Where do you feel you could improve—either at the sentence level (style, voice, rhythm) or structurally (pacing, tension, character arcs, etc.)?
4. Do you want exercises, real-time feedback on your writing, discussion of theory, or a mix?

✍️ Step 2: Choose a Focus

Based on your answers, we can dive into any of these areas:

- **Narrative Precision** – Sharpening character motivation, plot structure, scene rhythm.
- **Stylistic Refinement** – Diction, syntax, paragraph flow, tone control.
- **Voice Calibration** – Strengthening a distinct voice across narrative or nonfiction modes.
- **Revision Strategies** – High-impact edits that improve clarity and power.
- **Deep Reading Practice** – Using excerpts from great authors to sharpen your own eye.

🛠️ Step 3: Practice and Feedback

We can do:

- Weekly craft drills or writing challenges.
- Critique sessions with feedback on your work.
- **Socratic dialogues** to push your thinking about technique.
- Real-time revision walkthroughs.

Would you like to start with a short diagnostic to set the direction? Or do you already have a project in progress I can help with?

I highly recommend that all writers establish a "writing coach" of their own.

Flipped Interaction Pattern

By default, we, the users, are in control of our conversations with the LLM. We take the initiative to ask questions or instruct it to do something for us. The Flipped Interaction pattern, however, reverses that dynamic: the LLM asks *us* questions. It works like this: We tell the model what we want it to do, then we tell it to ask *us* questions, gather all of our answers, and use the answers to create a solution for our initial request.

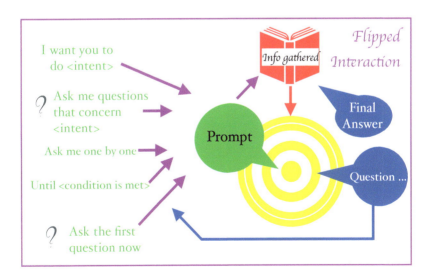

Key phrases: *Ask me questions that concern <intent>, Ask me one by one, Until <condition is met>, Ask the first question now; Interview me*

This pattern can be used for mock interviews,[5] gathering information to write a report, collecting data for analysis, etc.

Here is an example of a conversation using the Flipped Interaction Pattern:

> Me: I would like to know the genre of the book I am working on. Please ask me questions one by one to help me. Try to ask as few questions as possible. Ask me the first question now.
>
> ChatGPT: Sure! Here's the first question: Does your book focus more on realistic events or include elements of the fantastical (magic, supernatural beings, advanced technology beyond our current world, etc.)?
>
> Me: Realistic
>
> ChatGPT: Got it! Is the primary focus on personal relationships and emotions, or does it center around external events like crime, politics, or historical events?
>
> Me: Historical person
>
> ChatGPT: Interesting!
> Is the book a fictionalized account of this historical person's life, or is it a nonfiction biography?
>
> Me: Nonfiction biography
>
> ChatGPT: Got it!

---

[5] See an example of a mock interview with an LLM in Marketing & Book Promotion.

Does the biography focus on the subject's entire life, or does it concentrate on a specific period or achievement?

Me: Entire life to the extent we can find info

ChatGPT: Understood!
Is the biography more academic and heavily researched, or is it written in a more narrative, engaging style for a general audience?

Me: Heavily researched with a narrative style

ChatGPT: Your book falls under **narrative nonfiction biography,** combining scholarly research with storytelling techniques to engage readers while maintaining historical accuracy.

Final question: Does the book primarily analyze the subject's personal life, their public achievements, or both equally?

Me: Both

ChatGPT: Your book is best classified as a **narrative nonfiction biography,** blending historical analysis with engaging storytelling to present both the personal and public life of the subject. It likely appeals to readers interested in well-researched, yet immersive biographies rather than purely academic studies.

Would you like recommendations for comparable biographies or authors in this style?

As you see from this dialogue, my answers drove the questions that the LLM asked. Sometimes, the LLM gave me a choice of responses, yet I responded with something entirely different. The LLM accepted this unexpected turn and continued on. Also note that I didn't define an end-state for the conversation. The model determined the point at which it had the information it needed and gave me the answer.

Sometimes when you ask an LLM to do a task, you don't know all of the information the LLM needs. In this case, you can use Flipped Interaction to elicit from the LLM any information required for an accurate and appropriate answer.

Game Play Pattern[6]

Have you ever wanted to experiment with a storyline by trying out alternative scenarios or dialogue? Perhaps you have been curious about how your story would have changed if your main character had turned right instead of left. By using the Game Play pattern, you can create engaging interactive experiences with alternative scenarios imagined as a game.

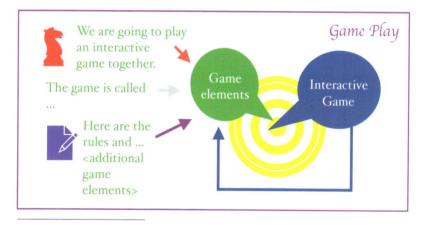

---

[6] Remarkably, most LLMs can play almost any game you know. You might want to test this. It can play thousands of games: board, card, video, table-top, traditional folk games, puzzles, mathematical, and even historical games. Ask the LLM about what games it knows. The response is impressive. This isn't the purpose of the Game Play pattern, although it is an interesting tidbit.

Key phrases: *We are going to play an interactive game together, Create an interactive game for me that concerns <x>,*
These are the game elements..., These are the mechanics (rules), . . .

To apply this pattern, you begin by telling the LLM that you are going to play an interactive game together. Then you proceed to explain the scope of the game that may include the theme, players, rules, and other essential elements. The key to this pattern is that the LLM drives the game play. It will apply its knowledge to guide the generation of content, prompting you to interact with it.

As a writer, this is a powerful pattern to help you explore story elements that you're developing. For instance, let's say you want to experiment with different **story arcs,** making decisions that alter the trajectory of a character's journey. To do this, you design a prompt using the Game Play pattern that sets up an interactive game where you make decisions for a character that dynamically impact the story structure, creating a branching narrative.

Or a simpler example: let's say you want to quiz yourself on writing techniques. You can design a game quiz as follows:

> Me: Let's play an interactive game together. You will write a sentence in passive voice and ask me to rewrite it in active voice. Then you will critique my effort. Do this for three sentences.

> ChatGPT: Great! Let's start. Here's the first sentence in passive voice:
> 1. The grand banquet was prepared by the finest chefs in the city.

> Now, rewrite it in active voice.

Me: The finest chefs in the city prepared the grand banquet.

ChatGPT: Excellent! Your sentence correctly shifts the focus to the doers of the action—the finest chefs. The structure is natural and maintains the original meaning perfectly.

Here's the second sentence:
2. A valuable painting was stolen from the gallery by an unknown thief.

Now, rewrite it in active voice.

Me: An unknown thief stole a valuable painting.

ChatGPT: Well done! You correctly placed the subject (*an unknown thief*) at the beginning, making the sentence more direct and engaging. The only slight difference is that "from the gallery" was left out. For full precision, you could write:

➡ An unknown thief stole a valuable painting from the gallery.

Now for the third sentence:
3. The final decision was made by the board after hours of discussion.
Rewrite it in active voice.

Me: After hours of discussion, the board made the final decision.

ChatGPT: Perfect! You preserved the meaning while making the sentence more direct and natural. Placing *after hours of discussion* at the beginning adds a smooth flow, emphasizing the process before the action.
Great job on all three! Want to play another round, or try a different challenge?

Later in this book, I will share with you some prompts that make use of Game Play pattern to experiment with narratives.

As I mentioned in a previous chapter, LLMs don't always provide perfect, infallible information. They generate responses based on patterns in their training data, but when they encounter gaps, they *hallucinate*—producing answers that sound plausible but may not be true.

Imagine this: You're a four-year-old prodigy with an uncanny ability to pull information from a cloud that follows you everywhere. When someone asks a question, you reach into the cloud, search for a matching pattern, and provide an answer. Everyone in your town is dazzled by your brilliance.

One day, a stranger from a distant land arrives, eager to test your knowledge. He quizzes you about the customs of his homeland—but your cloud has no data on this! You're four, so you shrug, giggle, and piece together an answer from the closest match you can find. It sounds reasonable, but it's wrong. The stranger, unimpressed, calls you a fraud and stomps off, never to return.

This is exactly the position that frontier LLMs are in. They can only generate responses based on what they've been trained on. When they don't have the right information, they still produce an answer[7]—because a next word can always be chosen based on probability. Whether it's true is irrelevant to the process.
So, how do we navigate this? How do we minimize the risk of misinformation?

---

[7] These are called "hallucinations."

We have patterns to help with this. I will show you two: Fact-Check List and Reflection.

Fact-Check List Pattern

To enhance the reliability of a response, you can use the Fact-Check List pattern. Basically, this pattern asks the LLM to list the core facts in a response that it just generated that would undermine the veracity of an answer if they were wrong. You can then review those facts and determine whether or not they are accurate.

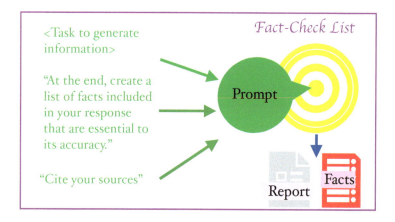

Key phrases: *At the end, create a list of facts included in your response that are essential to its accuracy (or that I should verify), Cite your sources*

Here is a conversation that illustrates this pattern and its effect:

> Me: Summarize the key causes of the Great Fire of 1835 in New York City. After your explanation, provide a list of key factual claims that I should verify.

ChatGPT: **Summary:**

The Great Fire of 1835 in New York City was caused by a combination of **dry weather, strong winds, and inadequate firefighting resources**. The blaze began in a warehouse in Lower Manhattan and rapidly spread, destroying nearly **700 buildings** and causing an estimated **$20 million in damage**. The lack of a municipal water system at the time hampered fire-fighting efforts, leading to widespread devastation.

☐ Fact-Check List:
- The fire started in a warehouse in Lower Manhattan.
- Nearly 700 buildings were destroyed.
- Damage was estimated at $20 million.
- There was no municipal water system in NYC at the time.

You might ask, what should you do with this list of facts? First, you review each fact. Then you cross-check them with trusted sources. If there are mistakes or gaps, refine your prompt with specific constraints such as "cite your sources" or "only include facts supported by peer-reviewed studies". If the facts are all correct, proceed. If not, either manually edit and correct or re-prompt the LLM with additional information or constraints.

Reflection Pattern

Another pattern designed to enhance the reliability and coherence of responses is the Reflection pattern. With this pattern, we will ask the LLM to reflect on its answer. This may seem like a cognitive impossibility since the LLM has no self-awareness. It is, however, able to predict what it's reflection might be, thereby making this an effective pattern.

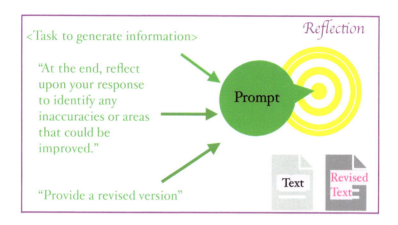

Key phrases: *At the end, reflect upon your response to identify any in accuracies or areas that could be improved, Provide a revised version.*

I regard this pattern as rather remarkable in that we are asking the LLM to reflect on its own work and then evaluate it and double-check it. And believe it or not, it is very effective. I have found that after using this pattern, the LLM will look at its responses critically and revise accordingly.

Here is how this works:

Me: Please write one paragraph that explains why Agatha Christie disappeared for a week. At the end, reflect upon your response to identify any inaccuracies or areas that could be improved. Provide a revised version.

ChatGPT: In December 1926, Agatha Christie vanished for eleven days, triggering a massive search involving police, volunteers, and even fellow authors like Sir Arthur Conan Doyle. Her disappearance followed a period of deep personal distress—her mother had recently died, and her husband, Archie Christie, had confessed to an affair and asked for a divorce. On the night of December 3, she left her home in Berkshire and abandoned her car near a chalk quarry in Surrey, sparking fears of suicide or foul play. She was eventually found at the Swan Hydropathic Hotel in Harrogate, Yorkshire, where she had checked in under the name "Teresa Neele," the surname of her husband's mistress. Christie never fully explained her disappearance, leading to widespread speculation. Some believe she experienced a fugue state or dissociative amnesia, while others suspect she staged the event to embarrass her husband or escape emotional turmoil.

Reflection on Accuracy & Areas for Improvement:

1. **Duration:** I initially said she disappeared for a "week," but she was actually missing for **eleven days**—this should be corrected.
2. **Car location:** Her car was abandoned **near Silent Pool in Surrey**, not simply "a chalk quarry."
3. **Hotel name:** The correct name of the hotel where she was found is **the Old Swan Hotel** (formerly Swan Hydropathic Hotel).
4. **Place of departure:** She left her home in **Sunningdale, Berkshire**, not just "Berkshire."
5. **Theories:** While dissociative amnesia and emotional distress are widely discussed, the idea of staging the disappearance for revenge is more speculative and should be stated more carefully.

Revised Version:

In December 1926, Agatha Christie disappeared for eleven days, sparking a nationwide search that involved police, volunteers, and even Sir Arthur Conan Doyle. Her sudden disappearance followed intense personal struggles—her mother had recently died, and her husband, Archie Christie, had admitted to an affair and requested a divorce. On the evening of December 3, she left her home in Sunningdale, Berkshire, and abandoned her car near Silent Pool in Surrey, with personal belongings inside. Her whereabouts remained unknown until she was discovered at the Old Swan Hotel in Harrogate, Yorkshire, where she had checked in under the name "Teresa Neele," the surname of her husband's mistress. Christie never publicly explained her disappearance, fueling ongoing speculation. While some believe she suffered from dissociative amnesia or a psychological breakdown, others suggest she fled to escape personal distress.

Would you like me to adjust the tone or emphasize certain aspects differently?

As I have mentioned, conversations with LLMs should typically be iterative. You'll go back-and-forth for as many iterations as you'd like. The Reflection pattern is particularly conducive to dialogue.

Other phrases that you can use to encourage the model to think critically about its responses include:

"Are you sure?"
"What assumptions did you make?"
"How confident are you in this response?"
"Did you include all of the facts?"
"Are there any weaknesses."

Patterns give us a way to work smarter with LLMs, not harder. As writers, we love to craft characters, shape narratives, and explore possibilities. Patterns let us do the same with AI—define roles, set the scene, and guide the interaction to get the response we actually need. Fact-checking, refining outputs, and structuring ideas all become more intuitive when we use the right approach.

At the end of the day, a well-designed prompt is like a well-placed key—it unlocks the response you're looking for.

Now that we've explored these patterns, let's put them into action.

Augmented Prompting

Consider this scenario: you have a document (in pdf format on your hard drive), the contents of which are a scholarly paper written in French. You need this information for a talk you will be presenting. You don't have access to a translator, but you do have a reliable assistant, your LLM.

You start a new conversation with your LLM. The first thing you do is upload the file into the LLM's memory[8]. When you see it has been accepted, you prompt it as follows:

> Me: Greetings! I have uploaded a document written in French.[9] Please read the paper, section by section from beginning to end. As you finish each section, translate the words into English. At the end, give me the full English version of the document.
>
> ChatGPT: Greetings! I've started reviewing the document and translating it section by section. Here's the **first translated section**:
>
> History of the Nativity Scene According to a Recent Work

---

[8] Most frontier models have the capacity to upload files. Press the "+" or *paperclip icon* near the prompt line and select the file that you want to upload.

[9] Mols, R. *Histoire de la crèche de Noël d'après un ouvrage récent*

By Roger Mols, S.J.
The Christmas nativity scene belongs simultaneously to
Christian art, religious ...

This continues for each section of the paper. After all of the text is successfully translated, I can now copy the translated version, edit it, or ask the LLM questions about the contents. For instance:

Me: In one paragraph explain what the paper believes to be the main factor in the origin of the nativity scene.

ChatGPT: The paper argues that the true origin of the Christmas nativity scene lies not in any single event or religious order—such as the oft-cited 1223 celebration by Saint Francis of Assisi—but in the gradual convergence of various devotional and artistic traditions that culminated around the mid-16th century. It emphasizes that the nativity scene, as we know it—a realistic, three-dimensional, emotionally engaging, and temporarily displayed tableau—emerged spontaneously and relatively late in Christian history. Its development was driven by the desire to foster intimate spiritual participation in the mystery of Christ's birth, particularly through visual realism that evoked presence and emotion. Among the influential forces promoting its spread were religious orders like the Jesuits, who, while not inventing the form, played a major role in popularizing it across Europe and missionary regions.

Me: According to the paper, what is the proper set-up of a nativity scene?

ChatGPT: According to the paper, a proper nativity scene is not just a decorative display or artistic creation—it is a **spiritual and psychological experience** designed to foster deep **emotional participation** in the mystery of Christ's birth. It must be a **realistic, three-dimensional**

representation arranged within a **real spatial setting**, creating the illusion that the viewer is personally present at the scene. The goal is to evoke what the Germans call *Miterlebnis*—a sense of shared experience—by depicting the figures as lifelike and natural as possible, without theatricality, symbolism, or exaggerated artistry. It should be **temporary**, constructed for the Christmas season in response to the liturgical cycle, and created with the intention of being **a prayer in action**, a spiritual offering that allows the viewer to "relive" the Nativity in a humble, reverent way.

Me: No symbolism?

ChatGPT: Great catch—and an important nuance.

The paper does **not** say that all symbolism is forbidden in a nativity scene, but it **warns against symbolism that overshadows the primary goal**: to create a realistic and emotionally immersive experience of the Nativity. The author emphasizes that the purpose of a nativity scene is *not* to impress through "technical virtuosity, outstanding artistic qualities, esoteric language, or symbolism." In other words, **symbolism is not the focus**—especially if it becomes abstract or distracts from the humble, human mystery being represented.

That said, traditional nativity scenes *often do include symbolic elements*—like the ox and donkey (symbolizing the Gentiles and Jews, or warmth and humility), or the star guiding the Magi. These are permitted as long as they **serve the realism and spiritual participation** of the viewer, rather than turning the scene into an intellectual or artistic puzzle. So it's not a rejection of all symbolism—just a reminder to **prioritize the devotional experience** over symbolic complexity.

Would you like a list of traditional symbols found in nativity scenes and their meanings, framed in line with this perspective?

44

Obviously, the model is chattier than I am. I have found that if I keep my prompts succinct and leave out filler words, the model has better focus.

Attaching items such as documents, images, and spreadsheet data to our prompt is a technique called Augmented Prompting. This technique provides the model with information to prioritize during the development of a response. Augmented Prompting is a type of manual Retrieval Augmented Generation, a technique where you access an external database to directly feed the LLM with data.

When you instruct the LLM to read the document, it loads the contents into its workspace (context window). At this point, you query the LLM against this information. You can literally ask any question about the contents of the file that you can think of.

You can also ask the LLM to create content based on the information in the file. For instance, you might want a summary, an outline, an extraction of the key terminology, a list of key points, a list of opinions expressed, a timeline, or a table of characters and their interactions.

5 The Writer's Assistant

I like to write notes on scraps of paper—ideas for stories, dialogue that I have heard, things people have told me, snippets from books, things I want to do, etc. It's a bad habit because I find myself hoarding scraps of paper with valuable notes on them.

You may have guessed: I can't always find that bit of paper when I need it.

I began this book as I usually do, with an outline, on a piece of paper — front and back. Here it is:

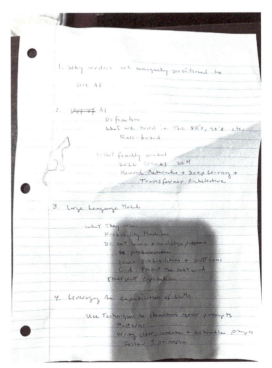

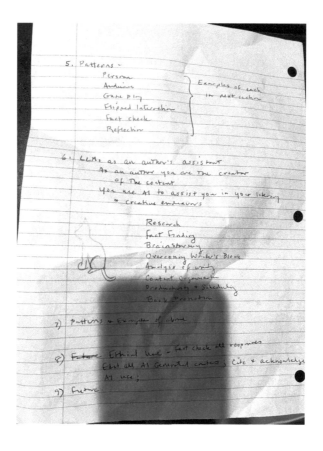

It's not easy to read. My handwriting is in archaic cursive—on crumpled paper. The shadow of my phone looms prominently in the lower center obscuring words. Altogether, this is not something my students would welcome reading.

I took photographs of each side of the paper and uploaded them into a multimodal LLM.[10]

---

[10] A multimodal LLM can handle different types of input and output: text, images, audio files, etc.

Me: Greetings! I have uploaded two documents. Please tell me what you can see.

ChatGPT: I can see two images of handwritten notes on lined paper. These notes appear to be an outline for a talk or a workshop related to AI and its applications for writers. Here are the key points from your notes:
Page 1:

1. Why writers are uniquely positioned to use AI
2. Definition of AI
   - What we tried in the '80s, '90s, etc. (Rule-based approaches)
   - What finally worked (2022 OpenAI LLMs)
   - Neural networks + deep learning + transformer architecture
3. Large Language Models (LLMs)
   - What they are
   - Probability machines
   - Do not learn knowledge/terms, they learn probabilities
   - Goal: Predict the next word
   - Emergent capabilities
4. Leveraging the capabilities of LLMs
   - Use techniques to structure your prompts
   - Patterns
   - Write clear, concise, actionable prompts
   - Follow three principles
Page 2:
5. Patterns
   - Persona
   - Audience
   - Game Play
   - Flipped Interaction
   - Fact-Check
   - Reflection
   - Examples of each in the next section
6. LLMs as an Author's Assistant
   - The author remains the creator of content
   - AI assists in literary and creative work
   - Use cases:

48

- Research
- Fact-finding
- Brainstorming
- Overcoming writer's block
- Analysis of writing
- Content organization
- Productivity & scheduling
- Book promotion
7. Patterns & examples of the above
8. Ethical Use
   - Fact-check all responses
   - Edit all AI-generated content
   - Cite and acknowledge AI use
9. Future

Additionally, I notice small sketches of a cat on both pages. Would you like me to format this into a structured digital outline?

Not only did the LLM transcribe my notes accurately, it recognized my crude attempts at drawing a cat in silhouette. At the end of its response, it took the initiative and asked me if I wanted it to format it in a structured digital outline. I replied, "Yes". *Et voilà!* The writing of this book commenced.

Meet your new personal assistant!

If you compare the outline above with the table of contents of this book, you will note many differences. My notes and the LLM's transcription were simply a starting point for me. As with all assistants, when I give mine a task, I look at the results and evaluate them. If the results are a 90% solution, I am thrilled. I know I still have work to do but I have just saved much time and effort. I have moved forward.

If the results are closer to a 60% solution, then I have to rethink my prompt or determine whether or not the task is suited to the skills of my assistant. In any case, having a personal assistant to help with some of the tasks in my daily workflow is a Godsend.

The life of a wordsmith is a life of a multi-talented individual. Not only do you have to have a solid grasp of all that goes into the writer's craft, but you also must know how to do research, pull ideas out of thin air, analyze and critique writing, and organize reams of paperwork and files. You have to be an expert at juggling a complex schedule, which at times may include immersing yourself into the unknown for the sake of your writing.

Once you have completed a piece for publication, you are swiveled into the dazzling world of promotion and marketing. This could mean that you learn how to build a website, or work social media, or spend many lovely hours on book tours. I could continue, but you get the point.

How can an LLM help? First, determine the tasks that are must-dos and can be facilitated by a capable assistant. Think about research, brainstorming new ideas, editing, scheduling, and marketing.

The next chapter offers sample prompts and accompanying conversations for six distinct writing tasks in which LLMs can provide support. You will notice that most of the initiating prompts use one or more prompt patterns.

Me: I have uploaded a hand-drawn map.

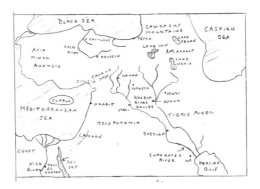

Me: Please recreate it and make it look like it's on parchment. Label it Land of the Hurrians.

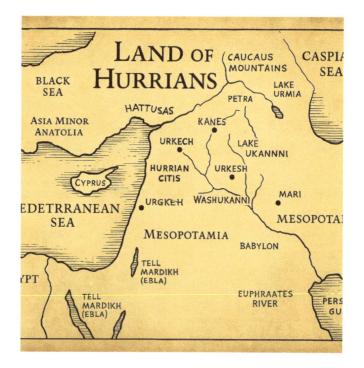

6 A Pocketful of Prompts

Research & Fact Finding

LLMs are able to perform an astonishing array of tasks to enrich the research process. Imagine having a subject matter expert at your right hand with whom you may ask any question at any time of day. This expert is capable of performing a wide range of tasks for you, from reviewing and summarizing documents to comparing and contrasting different source materials.

1. Summarizing texts

Patterns: Persona
Structural Techniques: Augmented Prompting
Prompt Example:

> Me: Good evening. Please act as a historian of Ancient Pre-Mesopotamia. I have uploaded a document[11] about the Hurrians. Please read it from beginning to end. Give me a tight outline of the major points covered in the paper.
>
> ChatGPT: Good evening!

---

[11] Hooper, T., Echoes of the Hurrians: Tracing an Ancient People from the Caucasus Mountains to Celt-Iberia to the Spanish New World

Here's a tight outline of the major points covered in the document on the Hurrians and their relation to ancient Iberians:

I. Purpose and Perspective
- Written from the viewpoint of a Spanish-American woman exploring ancestral origins.
- Argues a significant genetic and cultural contribution to Spanish ancestors by peoples from the Caucasus—specifically the Hurrians.

II. Origin and Identity of the Hurrians
- Hurrians originated in the Caucasus foothills.
- Known for metallurgy, horse domestication, irrigation systems, laws, and musical composition.
- Their homeland was often called "Land of the Hurrians" despite various other regional names.

III. Iberian Connection
- Ancient Iberia (in the Caucasus) and Celt-Iberia (in Spain) are linked by migration.
- DNA and archaeological evidence support a migration from the Georgian Caucasus to the Iberian Peninsula around 2500 BC.
- Migrants may have arrived via Phoenician ships, eventually influencing Spanish genetic and cultural development.

IV. Cultural Contributions
- Early use and trade of copper, tin, and silver.
- Spread of metallurgy and horse-based warfare (chariots).
- Widespread cultural influence: law, religion, music (e.g., Ugarit texts), and language.
- They were absorbed into larger civilizations but retained cultural influence through the Mitanni and later Urartu.

V. Linguistic and Mythological Traces
- Eastern Caucasian languages may descend from Hurrian-Urartian roots.

- Stories from Greek mythology (e.g., Prometheus, Medea, the Golden Fleece) set in Colchis hint at Hurrian cultural memory.
- The name "Iberia" may derive from the Biblical figure Eber, linking both Eastern and Western Iberias.

VI. Historical Chronology Highlights
- **6000–3000 BC:** Tell Halaf and Tell Brak cultures; early metallurgy.
- **2600–2000 BC:** Expansion into Mesopotamia; horse training; links to Akkadian and Sumerian cultures.
- **1900–1300 BC:** Rise of Mitanni kingdom (Hurrian-led); interactions with Egypt; Amarna Letters.
- **1300–600 BC:** Fall of Mitanni; Urartu (Vannic state) rises; cultural absorption into Assyria and Persia.
- **300–30 BC:** Hellenistic fusion post-Alexander; Kartli kingdom (Georgia); name Iberia persists.
- **100–888 AD:** Iberia sees Roman and Persian influence; converts to Christianity; later becomes United Georgia.

VII. Biblical and Historical Reflections
- Parallels drawn between Hurrians and Biblical Horites.
- Old Testament practices (e.g., Sarah and Hagar) may reflect Hurrian legal customs.
- Solomon's Tarshish fleet and the metallurgical links to Spain are emphasized.

VIII. Conclusion: Interwoven Identities
- Hurrians may have been the progenitors or major contributors to the Iberians.
- Their traits—resilience, skill in metallurgy and horsemanship, adaptability—persist in cultural memory.
- Their name and identity evolved but left lasting marks on language, law, and lineage.

The paper that I uploaded was a dense 22-page excerpt from a monograph written by a paleography-trained genealogist. As you see, the outline is fascinating. Now, I wanted to see a timeline.

Me: Please create a timeline of the key events.

ChatGPT: Here is a visual timeline highlighting key events in Hurrian and Iberian history, from early Mesolithic settlements through the unification of the Georgian monarchy in 888 AD. Let me know if you'd like a version you can download or a map of their migration next.

Timeline of Key Events in Hurrian and Iberian History

13,000-8000 BC	Early settlement in Caucasus (Mesolithic–Neolithic)
6000-5000 BC	Tell Halaf/Brak culture and early metallurgy
3500 BC	Discovery of copper and Chalcolithic metallurgy in Caucasus
3000 BC	Urkesh city established; Hurrians in Mesopotamia
2600-2100 BC	Hurrians take over Nagar (Tell Brak); horse training manuals appear
2500 BC	Migration from Caucasus to Iberian Peninsula
2300 BC	Earliest Hurrian written texts in Anatolia
2000 BC	Hurrian language used in Ugarit; Hurrians in Mari
1900-1200 BC	Hurrian expansion; Mitanni kingdom established
1500-1400 BC	Hurrian cultural influence peaks; Amarna Letters
1275 BC	Assyrians destroy Mitanni capital; decline begins
1200-600 BC	Urartu/Vannic Kingdom dominates; Hurrian legacy persists
600 BC	Greek references to Caucasus region as Iberia
302 BC	Pharnavaz becomes first king of Kartli (Iberia)
334 AD	Christianity becomes state religion in Iberia
888 AD	Unification into United Georgian Monarchy

This chart was produced in a blink of an eye and saved as a .png image for me in my /downloads directory. I could readily import it into this document. At this point, there are many paths I may pursue, many questions I may ask. For instance:

> Me: Please extract the most important quotation and provide a one-sentence commentary.
>
> ChatGPT: **Most Important Quotation**
>
> "The people who developed metallurgy in the Caucasus traveled by Phoenician ships to the area of ore-laden mountains to extract the copper and other metals and to smelt the ore in a land now known as Spain, or the Celt-Iberian Peninsula."
>
> **Commentary:**
> This line crystallizes the central thesis that the technologically advanced Hurrians migrated westward and became a foundational force in the cultural and genetic makeup of ancient Spain.
>
> Me: Is this plausible?
>
> ChatGPT: Excellent question—and it's both historically **provocative** and worth unpacking.
>
> ⏱ Is it plausible that Hurrians migrated to Spain and influenced the Celt-Iberians?
> **Short answer:**
> There is no direct, universally accepted evidence proving that the Hurrians themselves migrated to Spain. However, **elements of the claim are plausible**, especially when examined through a multidisciplinary lens (archaeology, genetics, linguistics, mythology). . . .

And so the conversation continues as the LLM and I volley back and forth until the wee hours of the night...

2. Research in the Wild

Prompting the LLM to answer research questions based on both its training data and external web sources is referred to as prompting "in the wild." The LLM is tapping into unverified sources whenever you prompt in the wild, therefore you should take extra cautions that the response you get is accurate. This is when the patterns, Fact-Check and the Reflection, come in handy.

It is also good practice to ask the LLM to cite its sources for later verification and to provide a list of references at the end, formatted according to your required citation style (MLA, APA, Chicago, IEEE, and so on).[12]

Patterns: Persona, Fact-Check
Structural Elements: Your intent, Output Structure, Task
Conversation Example:

> Me: Greetings! I am researching an ancient people known as the Hurrians (after their writing). Please act as a historian of ancient Mesopotamia. Provide me an overview of the Hurrians in two concise and well-structured paragraphs with specific details. For each fact stated, please give a citation. At the end give me the source list in Chicago format.
>
> ChatGPT: Greetings! Here's an overview of the Hurrians from the perspective of a historian of ancient Mesopotamia, with citations provided for each fact and a bibliography in Chicago format:

---

[12] The LLM can convert between formats.

The Hurrians were a significant non-Semitic, non-Indo-European people who emerged in northern Mesopotamia and the Upper Tigris-Euphrates region during the third millennium BCE. They spoke the Hurrian language, a linguistic isolate that shows no clear relation to other known ancient tongues, although it shares certain structural features with Urartian, suggesting a possible linguistic family (Wilhelm 1989, 1–3). By the mid-second millennium BCE, Hurrian influence had expanded through the establishment of city-states like Nuzi and the powerful kingdom of Mitanni, where Hurrian elites even governed an Indo-Aryan military aristocracy (Bryce 2005, 138–140). The Hurrians were instrumental in the transmission of cultural and religious ideas, especially into Hittite Anatolia, where Hurrian deities and mythologies, such as those of Teshub and Kumarbi, were incorporated into Hittite texts (Beckman 1999, 15–18).

Although politically fragmented for much of their history, the Hurrians left a lasting cultural impact. Archaeological findings from sites like Tell Mozan (ancient Urkesh) reveal sophisticated urban planning, palace structures, and religious architecture tied to Hurrian cults (Buccellati and Kelly-Buccellati 2002, 27–32). Their political influence peaked with the Mitanni kingdom (ca. 1500–1300 BCE), which acted as a regional power rivaling Egypt and the Hittite Empire until its decline due to internal strife and external pressures (Liverani 2014, 253–256). Though Mitanni eventually collapsed, the Hurrian legacy endured, especially through their myths and administrative practices preserved in Hittite archives at Hattusa and in Akkadian cuneiform throughout Mesopotamia (Singer 1999, 725–727).

Sources (Chicago Style):
- Beckman, Gary. *Hittite Diplomatic Texts*. Atlanta: Society of Biblical Literature, 1999.
- Bryce, Trevor. *The Kingdom of the Hittites*. Oxford: Oxford University Press, 2005.
- Buccellati, Giorgio, and Marilyn Kelly-Buccellati. "Urkesh and the North: Recent Discoveries." In *Ancient Syria: A Three Thousand Year History*, edited

by Trevor Bryce, 27–32. Oxford: Oxford University Press, 2002.

- Liverani, Mario. The Ancient Near East: History, Society and Economy. New York: Routledge, 2014.
- Singer, Itamar. "The Hittites and the Hurrians." In *Civilizations of the Ancient Near East*, edited by Jack M. Sasson, 727–736. New York: Charles Scribner's Sons, 1999.
- Wilhelm, Gernot. *The Hurrians*. Warminster: Aris & Phillips, 1989.
-

Would you like a visual timeline or map to go with this overview?

Me: Has more recent research been done or have more discoveries been made?

ChatGPT: Yes, recent research has significantly expanded our understanding of the Hurrians. In 2023, archaeologists working at the ancient site of Hattusa (the Hittite capital in modern-day Turkey) uncovered a new cache of cuneiform tablets containing Hurrian-language texts. One particularly intriguing discovery was a previously unknown ritual text written entirely in Hurrian—uncommon among surviving documents, which are often bilingual or in Akkadian. This suggests a deeper and more autonomous literary tradition than previously understood (Weiss, 2023).

Additionally, advances in digital epigraphy and linguistic reconstruction have allowed scholars to reevaluate Hurrian grammar and vocabulary with greater precision. A 2022 project funded by the German Research Foundation (DFG) used high-resolution imaging and computational analysis to revisit old Hurrian tablets from archives in Ugarit and Boghazköy. These efforts have contributed to an updated Hurrian dictionary and improved syntactic models, enabling a better understanding of Hurrian myths and rituals, such as the "Song of Kumarbi," which underlies much of Hittite religious literature (Jakob, 2022).

> Would you like a summary of the most recent findings formatted for use in a research paper or presentation?

The LLM continued to give me sources for each fact even though I didn't prompt it to do so. The LLM will "remember" your earlier instructions and apply them as appropriate.

Brainstorming Ideas

As a writer, I love to dream. I love to think of truly out-of-the-box ideas. I also create lists, many. I write random ideas on a blackboard where anyone can add or make comments. Brainstorming, whether solo or with others, is an important part of my creative process.

The LLM excels as a dynamic brainstorming partner, offering a constant stream of ideas to spark creativity. Have you ever heard the fairy tale called *Tina and the Magic Pot?*[13] In this story, our heroine, Tina, finds a pot that will fill with porridge indefinitely until she tells it to stop. I can't help but think of my LLM as a magic pot that will keep cooking a porridge of words until I say "Stop, magic model, STOP!"

When you ask the LLM to give you ideas, it will. However it is not like the magic pot where it will continue to spew ideas uncontrollably. Today it does stop. You can give it a specific number of ideas you want, but you have to be reasonable. A while back, I performed an experiment to see how far it would go. I

---

[13] Also known as *Sweet Porridge* or *Der süße Brei,* a German fairy-tale (Brothers Grimm), first published in 1815.

repeatedly asked it to give me ideas in chunks of twenty-five. It cooperated until about the 200th idea at which point it halted and wouldn't budge.

Theoretically, it will give you a limitless number of ideas.[14] In practice, you should ask for a reasonable number. In the following example I only ask for ten for the sake of publication. Take a look.

Patterns: Persona
Structural Elements: Context, Problem, Goal

> Me: Good evening. You are very creative. I am helping a friend write a memoir. She is trying to figure out how to organize it. She initially planned to tell her story chronologically, but that isn't working. Please brainstorm with me and give me 10 effective ways to tell the story of her life.
>
> ChatGPT: Good evening! Thank you—that means a lot. I'd be glad to brainstorm with you. Memoirs are so personal, and finding the right structure can make all the difference. If a chronological structure feels limiting or flat, here are 10 alternative (and effective) ways your friend could organize her story:
>
> 1. Thematic Structure
> Organize the memoir by themes (e.g., *Love, Loss, Resilience, Belonging, Faith*). Each chapter or section explores one theme through key memories, even if they jump in time.
> ✅ Great for weaving emotional threads and highlighting transformation over time.
>
> 2. Framed by a Central Event

---

14 Responses are limited by the length of the context window.

Use one major life event (e.g., a funeral, a diagnosis, a trip, a move) as the "present," and flash back from there to show what led up to it and what it means.

✅ Helps anchor the reader and adds narrative tension.

3. Circular or Full-Circle Structure

Begin and end with a similar scene or motif (a conversation, a place, an image), showing how the character has changed or what's been resolved in between.

✅ Emotionally satisfying and helps tie disparate experiences together.

4. Object-Based or Sensory Anchors

Each chapter centers around a specific object, photograph, smell, taste, or place that triggers a memory (like a family recipe, a dress, a scar, a scent).

✅ Excellent for evocative, sensory writing and symbolism.

5. Letter or Journal Format

Tell the story through letters to a child, partner, or younger self—or use journal entries to reveal thoughts and memories over time.

✅ Intimate and reflective; works well when the story has emotional nuance.

6. Milestone or Turning Points

Structure the memoir around defining moments: *first love*, *losing faith*, *meeting someone important*, *breaking away from something*.

✅ Keeps the narrative moving forward without needing to include every detail.

7. Before and After

Split the memoir into two main sections: *Before X* and *After X* (where X is a pivotal change—divorce, immigration, illness, awakening, etc.).

✅ Powerful if the life event truly created a 'before' and 'after' identity.

8. Geographical or Place-Based Structure
Organize the story by locations—*Grandma's house, boarding school, New York City, the garden*—with each place unlocking key memories.

✅ Great if a sense of place is integral to her identity.

9. Lessons Learned
Each chapter could be framed around a lesson learned or an insight gained, such as *"How I learned to forgive"* or *"Why silence matters."*

✅ Works well if the memoir has a reflective, philosophical tone.

10. Parallel Lives
Tell two timelines side-by-side: the life she lived vs. the one she dreamed of, or her inner life vs. outer reality—or even her own story paralleled with her mother's or daughter's.

✅ Adds emotional depth and complexity; useful for intergenerational themes.

Would you like help matching one of these to her specific story or struggles? Or is there a particular mood or message she's trying to get across?

Me: Oh, these are good ideas! Thank you.

ChatGPT: You're so welcome! I'm really glad they helped.
😊 If you'd like, we can play around with one of those structures using parts of her story to see what fits best—or even combine a couple of them for something unique. Just let me know what parts of her life she most wants to focus on, and I'll brainstorm further with you.

To encourage the LLM to give you good, relevant ideas, be certain to frame your prompt with specific context, as I did above. If none of the ideas the LLM offers are of interest, tell it you want more ideas—perhaps giving it additional directions.

Overcoming Writers' Block

What do you do when inspiration is elusive? How do you cope when the words won't come, your writing feels forced, your plot is boring, and your characters fall flat? You have to push forward, even though you feel stuck in molasses. You are a writer and writer's block is unfortunately part of the process—for most of us.

The LLM can nudge us out of our morass in both straightforward and playful ways. Here is a direct way to ask the LLM to help:

> Me: Greetings. It is a sunny afternoon and I have a deadline to write a short story and I don't feel like budging. I am stuck. I am not moving forward. How does a writer get out of this morass?

> ChatGPT: Greetings to you too. Sunny afternoons have a way of making deadlines feel like distant clouds—we see them, we know they're there, but we'd rather just bask. Still, you're in the thick of it, and I've got you.
> Here's a little rallying cry disguised as a set of practical, gentle nudges:
>
> **1. Lower the bar (on purpose):**
> Write the worst sentence you can imagine. Just one. Let it be terrible. In fact, make it absurd: "The banana wore a hat and refused to pay rent." Now that you've broken the seal, follow it with a slightly less bad sentence. You're moving.
> **2. Change the question:**
> Instead of asking "What should I write?" ask "What would amuse me right now?" or "What would happen if the most unexpected character entered the scene?"
> **3. Write a letter to yourself from your main character:**
> Let them talk to you. Let them say, "Hey, I'm bored too. I'm tired of standing around waiting for you. Want to run

64

off with me for just ten minutes?" Ten minutes. Set a timer.
Run.
4. Disrupt your environment, slightly:
Move to another chair. Write with a pen instead of typing.
Dictate a scene out loud while pacing. Even a symbolic
gesture can knock something loose.
**5. Call the story a sketch instead of a story, just for
now.**
Sketches aren't final. Sketches don't have to be good. But
sketches often surprise you and grow into things when
you're not looking.

If you'd like, I can prompt you with a quirky or dramatic
first line, a strange image, or even a complete story setup to
build from. Would that help shake things loose?
And lastly: you're not stuck. You're just waiting to take the
next step, and now you're a little closer to it. Let's take it
together.

This is such a warm and embracing response with valuable
insights. A few more interactions in this conversation and I'd
most likely be ready to carry on with my writing project.

Another technique, this one more intriguing and playful is to ask
the LLM to play a game with you that you have designed:

Me: Please design a game for authors. You will guide the
author out of writer's block. The game starts with you
asking the author a question tangentially related to their
work. Wait for the author's response. Then secretly think
of 6 strategies to help the author. Choose one strategy.
Implement the game. Occasionally give guidance using
advice from well-known authors. The game should be
interactive.

ChatGPT: Let's begin!
Here's your first question:
What is an object that appears frequently in your current
work, and why is it important?

Me: Sadness

ChatGPT: Interesting choice. **Sadness** as an object suggests it holds weight in your story—perhaps as an atmosphere, an emotion embedded in a character, or even as something tangible, like a letter, a song, or an heirloom. Now, I'll secretly select one of six strategies to guide you out of writer's block...

🌀 **Strategy Chosen: "Defamiliarization"** – This technique makes the familiar strange, allowing you to see your theme (sadness) from a fresh angle.
Your Challenge:
Describe sadness without using the word "sad" or any direct synonyms (e.g., sorrowful, miserable, etc.).

💡 **Tip from Ernest Hemingway:**
"Find what gave you the emotion; what the action was that gave you the excitement. Then write it down making it clear so the reader will see it too and have the same feeling."
Take your time. How would you describe sadness in your story without naming it?

Me: I guess sadness comes out in my writing because my life is generally happy.

ChatGPT: That's a fascinating insight—almost like sadness is a shadow cast by happiness, something you explore because it isn't dominant in your life. Many great writers do this, using fiction to engage with emotions they don't experience often or to examine them from a safe distance.

🔄 New Challenge: Flip the Perspective
Instead of describing sadness directly, describe happiness from the perspective of someone who doesn't trust it.

💡 **Tip from F. Scott Fitzgerald:**
"Show me a hero, and I'll write you a tragedy."
How would a character who has been hurt before experience happiness? Would they see it as fleeting? A trick? A quiet before a storm?

66

Me: H. was hurt by Annette when she chose not to go with him. Can he be happy with Eva?

ChatGPT: That's a compelling emotional conflict. H. has been wounded by Annette's choice. Now, with Eva, happiness is possible—but does he trust it? Or does he see it as a temporary illusion, something fragile that could vanish like before?

🎭 Your Next Challenge:
Write a short scene (just a few sentences) where H. is with Eva, experiencing a moment that should be happy—but something inside him holds back. Show us his hesitation without outright stating it.

💡 **Tip from Virginia Woolf:**
"The beauty of the world...has two edges, one of laughter, one of anguish, cutting the heart asunder."
How does H. react to happiness when he fears it might be taken away?

We can do this all day.

If you can't think of a game design, you can simply request the LLM to think of a game to help you out of writer's block. It will happily comply.

Editing, Analysis & Feedback

We are all writers in one capacity or another. Our goal is to communicate via the written word. No matter how much we believe our work is finished, it typically can always be improved. One of the amazing gifts that this technology brings is the full-time availability of an assistant who will read our work and help us critique and improve it. The feedback is instantaneous.

I can ask my LLM assistant if my text is too repetitive, too vague, or too difficult to understand. I can ask it if I use too many cliché's. Do I cover my subject adequately? Is the narrative consistent throughout? Are my characters believable? Do I have any plot holes? Any awkward phrasing?

Open any book on writing and composition. Every topic in that book—clarity, flow, organization, thesis, transitions— can be discussed with your LLM assistant.

Prompt Patterns: Persona

Here is an example:

> Me: Act as an editor. I have an introduction for an article on beehives. Please analyze it for engagement and clarity. Suggest three ways to improve it. Here is the text:

> Beekeeping, or apiculture, is the practice of maintaining honeybee colonies, typically in man-made hives, to produce honey, beeswax, and other products. It's not something you would typically do in large social groups, but rather a solitary task that requires patience and attention to detail. You'll need to familiarize yourself with the bees' behavior, learn how to care for the hive, and possibly harvest honey

at the end of the season. It's a low-key way to contribute to the environment and maybe even produce something sweet, although there's no rush. Everything happens slowly, and it's okay if you prefer to do it on your own terms.

ChatGPT: Your introduction does a good job of providing an overview of beekeeping, but there are some areas where you can enhance engagement and clarity. Here's a breakdown and three suggestions for improvement:

Analysis:
1. **Engagement:** The introduction starts with a simple definition, which is fine but may feel a bit dry. There is potential to draw in the reader by evoking more emotion or curiosity about the subject.
2. **Clarity:** Some phrasing could be streamlined for smoother reading. While the message is clear, breaking up longer sentences and simplifying language can help improve readability.
3. **Tone:** The tone feels calm and approachable, but it could be made more inviting and personal to create a stronger connection with the reader.

Suggestions:
1. **Add a hook to capture interest:** Begin with a more engaging or intriguing opening sentence that sparks curiosity. You could start with a question or an interesting fact about bees or honey production to immediately draw the reader in.
   Example: "Have you ever wondered where the sweet honey in your tea comes from? Beekeeping, or apiculture, offers a fascinating glimpse into the world of bees—and a rewarding hobby for those willing to learn."

2. **Simplify and tighten sentences:** Some sentences can be broken into shorter, more direct statements to improve readability. Streamlining phrasing can help keep the flow engaging without overwhelming the reader.
   Example: "Beekeeping involves maintaining

69

honeybee colonies in man-made hives to produce honey, beeswax, and other products. It's a solitary task that requires patience and a deep understanding of bee behavior. As you care for the hive, you'll also learn how to harvest honey at the end of the season."

3. **Incorporate sensory or emotive language:** Engage the reader by adding more sensory or emotional language that connects them to the experience of beekeeping. This could help create a sense of connection and empathy with the subject. **Example:** "Beekeeping is a peaceful, slow-paced endeavor that lets you connect with nature. As you watch the bees work, you'll feel the satisfaction of contributing to the environment, all while producing something sweet and natural."

These adjustments can help make the introduction more engaging, clear, and inviting, offering readers a stronger reason to keep reading.

Here is another example: I write what I think is a lovely descriptive paragraph, and I ask for a critique from my writing group and, lo and behold, I am told that I have written most of my sentences in passive voice!

Me: Please look at the following paragraph. Change all passive voice sentences to active voice. Do not change the tone of the narrative.

"I opened the door to a room piled high with every imaginable type of bric-brac. That first view will always be remembered. With timidity, I entered not knowing what I might encounter. The darkness only made the situation more dreadful. I fumbled around until I found a switch and bright light flooded the room, casting deep shadows. I surveyed the situation. All of it would have to be organized and inventoried. First, however, the trash has to be collected and disposed immediately. The books will have to be dusted and carefully checked for bookworms. The stacks of dishes will have to be washed. The newspapers will go straight to the recycling. Perhaps the magazines can be bundled and put into a pile for the library. The figurines will be collected and researched. I mentally cataloged the amount of time it would take the team. As I took out my phone, a stack of books suddenly fell over." ###

ChatGPT: Here's the revised paragraph with all passive voice constructions changed to active voice, while keeping the tone and flow of the narrative intact:

I opened the door to a room piled high with every imaginable type of bric-brac. I will always remember that first view. With timidity, I entered not knowing what I might encounter. The darkness only made the situation more dreadful. I fumbled around until I found a switch and bright light flooded the room, casting deep shadows. I surveyed the situation. I would have to organize and inventory all of it. First, however, I need to collect and dispose of the trash immediately. I must dust the books and carefully check them for bookworms. I will wash the random stacks of dishes. I'll toss the newspapers. Perhaps I can bundle the magazines and put them into a pile for the library. I'll collect and research the figurines. I mentally cataloged the amount of time it would take the team. As I took out my phone to make notes, a stack of books suddenly fell over.

Me: In your version all of the sentences begin with "I". As you can see, near the end of the paragraph the narrator refers to a team. Do you think the narrator is working alone?

ChatGPT: Great observation—and you're right to question that detail. The original paragraph subtly shifts from a solitary perspective ("I opened the door...") to a broader, shared effort ("it would take the team"). This implies the narrator is either preparing the space for a team or working as part of one. So, using "I" repeatedly for all the actions may not accurately reflect that context.

Let me revise the paragraph to reflect that nuance, varying sentence structure and attributing responsibility more appropriately across the narrator and the implied team:

I opened the door to a room piled high with every imaginable type of bric-brac. That first view will always stay with me. With timidity, I entered, not knowing what I might encounter. The darkness only made the situation more dreadful. I fumbled around until I found a switch, and bright light flooded the room, casting deep shadows. I surveyed the situation. Everything needed to be organized and inventoried. First, however, someone had to collect and dispose of the trash immediately. The team would need to dust the books and carefully check them for bookworms. Someone would have to wash the random stacks of dishes. The newspapers needed tossing. Perhaps we could bundle the magazines and stack them for the library. The figurines required collection and research. I mentally cataloged the amount of time the team would need. As I took out my phone to make notes, a stack of books suddenly fell over.

Me: Please show me how it looks if it were more formal.

ChatGPT: Absolutely. Here's the same paragraph revised for a more formal tone while maintaining the shift from individual to team involvement, and keeping all sentences in active voice:

I opened the door to a room filled with every imaginable type of bric-a-brac. That initial view remains vivid in my memory. With measured caution, I stepped inside, uncertain of what I might encounter. The darkness only heightened the sense of unease. After some fumbling, I located a switch, and bright light flooded the space, casting deep shadows along the walls. I took stock of the situation. The entire room would require thorough organization and inventory. As an immediate priority, the team would need to collect and dispose of the accumulated trash. The books required dusting and careful inspection for signs of bookworms. The assorted stacks of dishes needed to be

72

washed. Newspapers had to be discarded. The magazines, perhaps, could be bundled and set aside for the library. The figurines would need to be gathered and researched. I estimated the time the team would require to complete the work. Just as I retrieved my phone to begin taking notes, a stack of books toppled suddenly to the floor.

At first, the model transformed all of my passive sentences into active ones. After I asked the model to rewrite it in a more formal tone, it changed many of the sentences back to passive voice. It responded correctly to my instructions.[15]

This conversation doesn't need to end at this point. I could have asked it about the passive sentences or I could have given an entirely different task such as rewriting it for an elementary school-age audience, or in the past or present tense. Alternatively, I could have prompted:

Me: Please rewrite this from the perspective of the room. Only include details that the room could sense.

ChatGPT: Certainly. Here's a rewritten version of the paragraph from the perspective of the room, including only what the room itself could perceive—light, sound, movement, presence, and changes in atmosphere:

The door creaked open, allowing a shaft of light to pierce my dim stillness. Footsteps hesitated at the threshold, then crossed into me with caution. Shadows shifted as the intruder moved, brushing against boxes and teetering piles. A hand grazed the wall, found the switch. Light blazed to life, banishing the gloom and drawing deep shadows along my cluttered edges. Air stirred. The scent of old paper and dust lifted. Objects shifted—some gently, some with the scrape of ceramic against wood. A murmur of breath, a

---

[15] Passive is often used in formal writing to put the emphasis on the direct object, rather than the subject.

pause, the soft hum of thought. Then the faint tap and
glow of a phone screen. Without warning, one stack
collapsed in a clatter that echoed off my walls, briefly
restoring the silence that had long been mine.

When we prompt the model to transform the style, tone,
perspective, level, etc., of a piece of writing, it is performing *style
transfer*. This capability also gives the LLM the ability to mimic
styles of writing, such as writing in the style of Voltaire or
drafting a poem in the style of Walt Whitman.

Additional helpful prompts for editing and analyzing your writing
as suggested by my LLM assistant:

Clarity & Conciseness
- "Rewrite this paragraph to be clearer and more
  concise."
- "Find and remove redundant phrases in this text."
- "Identify any unnecessary filler words in this section."
- "Make this passage easier to understand for a general
  audience."
- "Rewrite this explanation at a 9th-grade reading level
  without losing meaning."

Structure & Flow
- "Analyze the logical flow of ideas in this paragraph.
  What could be rearranged?"
- "Do the ideas in this section build on each other
  effectively?"
- "Suggest transitions that would improve the flow
  between these paragraphs."
- "Does this introduction set up the rest of the chapter
  well?"
- "Mark any sentences that feel out of place or disrupt
  the rhythm."

💬 Tone & Voice

- "Adjust the tone of this passage to sound more professional (or more casual)."
- "Does the voice in this chapter feel consistent with earlier chapters?"
- "How do I make this dialogue sound more natural and true to each character."
- "Soften this critique without losing its message."
- "Is this section too emotionally flat? How can I add subtle emotion without overdoing it."

🧰 Grammar, Style, & Mechanics

- "Check this excerpt for grammar and punctuation errors."
- "Convert all passive voice to active voice where appropriate."
- "Standardize punctuation and formatting for consistency."
- "Identify any run-on or fragment sentences."
- "Does this text overuse certain words or sentence structures?"

🧭 Narrative & Character Revision

- "Does this chapter advance the character's arc? If not, what's missing?"
- "Evaluate the pacing of this scene—too fast, too slow, or just right?"
- "Are the stakes in this conflict clear and compelling?"
- "What parts of this chapter could be cut or condensed without losing meaning?"
- "Does this moment feel emotionally earned? If not, what would help?"

🔍 Thematic & Big Picture

- "What themes are emerging in this chapter? Are they consistent with the rest of the book?"
- "Does this ending reflect the main character's journey?"

- "Suggest revisions to make this conclusion more satisfying."
- "What unanswered questions remain for the reader at this point?"
- "Is the message of this essay/story clear? If not, how could it be sharpened?"

As you can see, any question about your writing that you would ask your critique group, your writing coach, your colleague, your beta reader, your professor, etc., you can ask the LLM.

Scheduling

Patterns: Persona, Flipped Interaction, Audience

Often, I work better when I have a schedule. I like to know what tasks I have looming over me and a timeline for getting them done. An LLM can be an engaging assistant for time-management.

Let's start with a weekly calendar. I initiate this process by creating a prompt with two patterns: Persona and Flipped Interaction. Persona gives my assistant a focus and Flipped Interaction tasks the model to ask me questions to develop an individualized plan.

> Me: Please act as a time-management expert. I need a weekly schedule to meet some challenging deadlines. Please create a schedule for me starting on Tuesday, March 24 and continuing through Saturday March 29 to manage my tasks. Ask me questions until you have enough information to develop an individualized plan. Ask me the first question now.

76

ChatGPT: Absolutely! I'm ready to help you create a focused, effective weekly schedule.

First question:
What are the specific tasks or projects you need to complete between Tuesday, March 24 and Saturday, March 29? Please include:
- A brief description of each task/project
- Any fixed deadlines or due dates
- Estimated time needed for each task
- Priority level (high/medium/low)

Once I have that, I'll ask about your availability and work style.

Me: Create video 1, 3 hours, due Saturday March 29, high priority; Create video 2, 3 hours, due Sat, high priority; Create video 3, 4 hours due Saturday. Create material for additional videos, 4 hours, due Saturday, high priority; Finish content for novel, 8 hours, due Thursday, highest priority; Write publicity blurb 1 hour due Wednesday, med. priority; I have a phone meeting on Tuesday from 11 to 1; I have another meeting on Friday from 11 to noon. I can do 2 hours of work before the meetings. I usually start work at 9 a.m.

ChatGPT:
Tasks & Deadlines

Task	Time	Due	Priority
Finish content for novel	8h	Thurs (Mar 27)	⭐ Highest
Create video 1	3h	Sat (Mar 29)	High
Create video 2	3h	Sat	High
Create video 3	4h	Sat	High
Create material for more videos	4h	Sat	High
Write publicity blurb	1h	Wed (Mar 26)	Medium

Fixed Commitments
- 📞 **Tues, Mar 24**: Phone meeting from **11 a.m. to 1 p.m.**
- 👩 **Fri, Mar 28**: Meeting from **11 a.m. to noon**
- You can work from 9 a.m. to 5 p.m. and 2 hours before meetings
- You prefer to start work at **9 a.m.**

Next question:
How many total hours per day are you realistically available to work?
(For example: Can you work 8 hours straight with breaks? Or do you prefer shorter, focused sessions throughout the day?)
Once I know that, I can structure your week around your energy and availability.

Me: 10 hours. I prefer shorter, focused sessions.

ChatGPT: Perfect—thanks! With your 10-hour workdays and a preference for **shorter, focused sessions**, I'll break each day into manageable blocks (e.g., 90 min sessions with breaks), prioritize deep work earlier in the day, and leave time for lighter or creative tasks later.
Before I build the schedule, I have one last question:
Do you prefer to focus on one major task per day, or would you rather switch between tasks (e.g., 2–3 different projects each day) to keep things fresh?

Me: Switch between tasks.

ChatGPT: Great! Since you're open to mixing tasks, I'll interleave deep work with creative and lighter tasks across the week. Here's a **custom weekly schedule** from **Tuesday, March 24 to Saturday, March 29** that:
- Honors your meetings
- Prioritizes your novel content early in the week
- Reserves focus time for video creation
- Keeps sessions short and balanced across your 10-hour workdays

- Leaves Saturday a bit lighter to account for flexibility or overflow

📝 Tuesday, March 24
Total work: 8 hrs (9–11, 1–7)

- **9:00–11:00**: ✍️ Novel content (2h)
- **11:00–1:00**: 📞 Phone meeting
- **1:00–2:30**: ✍️ Novel content (1.5h)
- 2:30–3:00: ☕ Break
- **3:00–4:30**: 📹 Video 1 (1.5h)
- **4:30–6:00**: 📹 Video 1 (1.5h)
- **6:00–7:00**: 🧠 Light admin / planning or optional wrap-up

📝 Wednesday, March 25
Total work: 10 hrs (9–7)

- **9:00–10:30**: ✍️ Novel content (1.5h)
- 10:30–11:00: ☕ Break
- **11:00–12:30**: ✍️ Novel content (1.5h)
- 12:30–1:30: 🍴 Lunch
- **1:30–2:30**: 📢 Write publicity blurb (1h)
- **2:30–4:00**: 📹 Video 2 (1.5h)
- **4:00–5:30**: 📹 Video 2 (1.5h)
- **5:30–7:00**: 📹 Create video 3 (1.5h)

📝 Thursday, March 26
Total work: 10 hrs (9–7)

- **9:00–10:30**: ✍️ Finish novel content (1.5h)
- 10:30–11:00: ☕ Break
- **11:00–12:30**: ✍️ Finish novel content (1.5h)
- 12:30–1:30: 🍴 Lunch
- **1:30–3:00**: 📹 Finish video 3 (2.5h total so far)

- **3:00–4:30**: 📽️ Video 3 (finish last 1.5h)
- **4:30–5:30**: 🧠 Brainstorm / begin material for additional videos (1h)
- **5:30–7:00**: 📽️ Continue material (1.5h)

📆 Friday, March 27
Total work: 9 hrs (9–6)
- **9:00–11:00**: 📽️ Finish material for additional videos (1.5h)
- **11:00–12:00**: 🙋 Meeting
- 12:00–1:00: 🍴 Lunch
- **1:00–2:30**: 📽️ Buffer / Polish video content (1.5h)
- **2:30–4:00**: 📽️ Catch-up or review (1.5h)
- **4:00–6:00**: 🧠 Optional overflow, review, relax

📆 Saturday, March 28
Optional Light Day: 6 hrs (9–3)
- **9:00–10:30**: Final touches on video projects (1.5h)
- **10:30–12:00**: Review everything, polish (1.5h)
- 12:00–1:00: 🍴 Lunch
- **1:00–3:00**: Final catch-up or rest

Would you like me to turn this into a printable format or calendar version?

At this point, you can work with the LLM to create the format that you prefer. I like lists, so this works for me.

Now, let's try an experiment. I am going to make full use of the Audience pattern to elicit from the LLM different ways it can help me with time management:

Me: Let's be creative. Let's say I am a writer who keeps all my notes in my head. I have an ambitious project and my head isn't big enough for it. I don't mesh with technology. I'll use pages on my mac and that's about it. How can you help me?

ChatGPT: I love this creative angle—and it's *so real* for many writers. Let's step into your shoes:

🧠✍️ You: A Writer with a Big Project and a Brain Full of Notes
- Your ideas live in your head
- You're **not techy** and don't want to learn fancy tools
- You use **Pages on your Mac**, maybe with folders, maybe not
- You've got a **big, ambitious project**—maybe a novel, a nonfiction book, or something sprawling
- But your brain is starting to feel like **a cluttered attic**, and you need a gentle, non-intrusive system

✨ Here's How I Can Help—Your Invisible Writing Assistant
1. I Help You Dump the Contents of Your Mind—Safely and Quickly
   - You just talk to me—stream of consciousness is *welcome*
   - I organize your thoughts into:
     - Chapters
     - Characters
     - Plot beats
     - Themes
     - Scenes or locations
     - Questions you're wrestling with

Think of me as your **external brain**, but I never tell you to install anything or download a weird app.

2. I Format Everything for Pages
- I give you clean, structured documents ready to paste into Pages
  (Want chapter outlines? A scene list? Character bios? A timeline? I'll make it.)

- I can also break big things into **bite-sized, page-friendly pieces**: one doc for plot, one for backstory, one for scenes.

3. I Help You Stay on Track—Without Techy Overwhelm
- I'll write you a **weekly writing plan**, like: "Write scene where Eliza finds the photograph—Target: 500 words, Due: Friday."
- I'll send you printable checklists or writing prompts you can paste at the top of your Pages doc.
- You can check in with me once a week: "Here's what I got done. What next?"

4. I Remind You What You Told Me
- "What color were the cliffs again?" I remember.
- "What was that idea I had about the narrator's secret?" I've got it saved.
- I'll hold your notes for you, and only show them when you ask. Like a **quiet writing partner** with a phenomenal memory.

5. I Celebrate Your Style
- No pressure to use AI-generated prose. You do the writing. I support your structure, timeline, and clarity.
- I help you stay grounded in **your voice**, your pace, and your unique method.

Want to Try?
Just tell me what's in your head. I'll gently help you pull out the pieces and turn them into a Pages-ready format.
You can say:
- "Here's what I know about my book so far…"
- "I have three characters and a twist ending—help me sort it."
- "This is too big—I don't know where to start."
Want to begin that brain-dump now?

Guess which option I chose?

Marketing & Book Promotion

Patterns: Persona, Audience, Flipped Interaction (Interview)

Researchers have found that GenAI is particularly good at developing persuasive content. This makes it well-suited for tasks related to marketing and book promotion. This includes drafting social media posts, author bios, taglines and hooks, press releases, and email newsletters. It is also adept at developing promotional assets, including book descriptions, advertising copy, and media one-sheets. If you give the LLM basic information about your project, you can prompt it to turn your input into a persuasive product.

Consider the following:

> Me: Greetings. I would like to introduce you to my character, Malcolm Reilly. Malcolm is a 45. year old man who has spent his life selling real estate. He has won the Golden Realtor award three times. He sells about a dozen high-end properties per year. He attended Colgate University and graduated with a degree in chemistry. He turned to real estate when he realized he needed a master's degree to do anything significant in the chemistry field. He loves selling historic properties. His hobbies include his horse farm where he tends to rescued horses. Please write a bio for Malcolm.

> ChatGPT: Certainly! Here's a professional bio for Malcolm Reilly that reflects his accomplishments, background, and personal interests:

> **Malcolm Reilly** is a distinguished real estate professional with over two decades of experience specializing in high-end and historic properties. A three-time recipient of the prestigious Golden Realtor Award, Malcolm is known for

his discerning eye, deep market knowledge, and personalized approach to every sale. He consistently handles a dozen exclusive properties each year, earning the trust of discerning clients who value discretion, taste, and integrity.

A graduate of Colgate University with a degree in chemistry, Malcolm initially pursued a career in the sciences before discovering his passion for real estate—a field that allows him to blend analytical precision with a deep appreciation for architecture and history. His particular love for historic homes has become a hallmark of his work, and he is widely respected for his ability to bring out the story and soul of every property he represents. When he's not helping clients find their perfect home, Malcolm can be found on his horse farm, where he rehabilitates and cares for rescued horses. The farm, a quiet sanctuary nestled in the countryside, reflects the same values that guide his professional life: dedication, patience, and a deep respect for tradition.

Would you like a more casual or personal version as well, or one tailored for a particular platform (like LinkedIn or a real estate agency's website)?

This result is a professional, well-constructed, and positive bio that accurately reflects the information I provided. Please note, the LLM also added details that I did not give it: "The farm, a quiet sanctuary nestled in the countryside." This is an assumption it made. It also assumed that Malcolm values "dedication, patience, and a deep respect for tradition." This is where human editing comes into play. My character, Malcolm, is actually a highly impatient person.

The next example is an exercise that I find worthwhile—the mock interview. In preparation for an upcoming interview, I turn to my LLM assistant. To set up the conversation, I'll use the patterns: Persona, Audience, and Interview (a sub-pattern of Flipped Interaction). Here's how this works:

> Me: I will be interviewed by a local journalist to discuss my newly released book, Conversing with AI: A Handbook for Writers. This book is the culmination of over a year of research and experimentation with generative AI and prompting methods. An important chapter concerns the right use of AI. Please play the role of interviewer & run a mock interview with follow-up questions based on my responses for a realistic rehearsal.

> GPT: Absolutely—let's get started with your mock interview. I'll ask questions like a local journalist would, and based on your responses, I'll follow up with realistic and relevant questions.

> ———

> **INTERVIEWER**:
> Thank you for taking the time to speak with me today. First, congratulations on your new book *Conversing with AI: A Handbook for Writers*. What inspired you to write this book?

> (Once you reply, I'll follow up accordingly.)

> Me: I was surprised and impressed when the first LLM was released to the public and I was determined to learn all that I could about this transformative technology.

> ChatGPT: **INTERVIEWER:**
> That curiosity really comes through in the book. Can you walk me through how you approached learning about large language models and what that process looked like over the year?

> (Did you take courses, run experiments, talk to other authors, or test different platforms? Your answer will shape the next follow-up.)

Me: I immediately made an account and started to play with it. There were limits at first. I watched youtube videos and then started to take short classes. I think the classes that made the biggest impact are the series of courses taught by Dr. Jules White of Vanderbilt University. I also took some IBM courses. Then I started to experiment with the techniques I learned.

ChatGPT: **INTERVIEWER:**
That's a thorough journey—and quite hands-on. What were some of the biggest surprises or breakthroughs you experienced once you moved from learning to experimenting? Was there a moment when you realized, "This could really change how authors work"?

Me: I experimented with the nuances of writing prompts and saw how prompt engineering techniques and the patterns discovered by the White Lab impact the response. Then I realized that writers, authors, wordsmiths were the ideal users of LLMs. After all, words are their expertise.

ChatGPT: **INTERVIEWER:**
That's a powerful insight—and one that really reframes the conversation around AI and creativity. Yet, many writers are still hesitant, even resistant. In your experience, what's the biggest misconception authors have about using AI, and how does your book address that?

Me: Perhaps they are afraid of two things: 1) The AI will steal their work, and 2) The AI will be better at writing than they are.

ChatGPT: **INTERVIEWER**:
Those are very real concerns. Let's take them one at a time. First, the fear that AI will steal their work—how do you address that in *Conversing with AI*? What should authors know about data privacy, intellectual property, and safe practices when working with these tools?

Me: That's a big topic. You need to read my book. In a nutshell, don't share data you want to keep private.

ChatGPT: **INTERVIEWER:** *(laughs)*
Fair enough! Good teaser. But seriously—your advice is simple and sound: don't share what you wouldn't want to be used or seen. Let's turn to the second fear you mentioned: that AI might be a better writer. How do you respond to that concern? Have you seen AI produce something that gave you pause, or do you see its role differently?

Me: I see AI as an assistant, a collaborator, a tutor. Yes, it writes well and is getting better all the time. It cannot, however, write what's in a person's heart. Thank you. Our time is up. I've enjoyed our talk!

ChatGPT: **INTERVIEWER:**
Beautifully said—"it cannot write what's in a person's heart." That really captures the spirit of your message. Thank you so much for your time today and for sharing your insights. I'm sure *Conversing with AI* will help many authors approach this technology with more confidence and creativity.

Best of luck with the book—and the many conversations it's sure to spark!

Would you like to run another round with a different tone —perhaps more technical, skeptical, or casual—or are you happy with this rehearsal?

Me: Please prepare a media one-sheet from this interview.

The mock interview, in itself, helped me prepare for a forthcoming interview. However, it also served another important purpose. After gathering the information from me, the LLM could then generate any marketing material I requested, in this case, a *media one-sheet*.

I edited the one-sheet and put it in Appendix III. This entire exchange, the interview and the production of the media sheet, took less than five minutes. Editing the media sheet took an additional fifteen minutes.

Writing copy and promotional material has always been a challenge for me. My copy typically reads either too dry or too forced. Therefore, when faced with the need to write persuasive copy, I readily turn to my assistant for the first draft. I don't often use the Interview pattern, however, I do use the Flipped Interaction pattern to give the model the information it needs. Consider this conversation to create back copy:

> Me: I am writing a book for authors about conversing with AI. Please ask me questions one at a time to gather information that you need to write back copy for me. Ask me the first question now.
>
> ChatGPT: Great—let's get started.
>
> First question:
> What is the primary benefit or transformation authors will gain by reading your book?
>
> Me: They will learn how to use AI as an assistant.
>
> ChatGPT: **Next question:**
> Is your book targeted at a specific type of author (e.g., fiction, nonfiction, self-published, traditionally published), or is it intended for all authors?

Me: All authors, writers, lawyers, journalists, poets, wordsmiths

ChatGPT: Perfect—broad but clearly language-focused professionals.
Next question:
What tone or style does your book use—professional, conversational, humorous, inspirational, etc.?

Me: Combination of professional, conversational

ChatGPT: Got it—balanced and approachable.
Next question:
Does your book include practical tools like prompts, exercises, templates, or case studies? If so, which ones?

Me: Prompts and case studies

ChatGPT: Great—very useful content.
Next question:
What makes your book different from other books about AI for writers? What's your unique angle or approach?

Me: I introduce a research-focused approach which includes structured prompting with prompt patterns and I discuss the right use of AI for authors.

ChatGPT: Excellent—structured prompting and ethical usage are strong differentiators.
Next question:
What stage of the writing or publishing process does your book focus on most—idea generation, drafting, editing, marketing, publishing, or all of the above?

Me: All

ChatGPT: Comprehensive—very appealing for a wide audience.
Next question:
What is the title (or working title) and subtitle of your book, if you have one?

Me: A handbook for Writers

ChatGPT: Strong and clear title.
Final question (for now):
Do you want the tone of the back cover copy to lean more persuasive (marketing-driven), informative (straightforward overview), or a blend of both?

Me: Blend with a slant towards informative

ChatGPT: Perfect. I have everything I need to draft your back cover copy. Here's a first version for your review: . . .

The LLM gave me a 95% solution. I was thrilled! Turn to the back cover of this book to read the final version.

Meanwhile another capability that you should explore when developing materials for promotion is image generation. Here are

Me: Show me a depiction of a radio DJ interviewing a writer. Make the writer a woman with short dark, chic hair style. Light complexion face. Professional clothes -- deep maroon jacket with a white linen blouse. Put some equipment in the background.

a few examples of what you can create with natural language prompts.

Me: Please make the same DJ as a five-year old.

Me: Nice. How does this look in Studio Ghibli style?

Me: Nice. How does this look in the style of cubism?

7 Using AI Responsibly & Ethically

What is the correct use of AI in our writing lives? This is a complex topic and an ongoing discussion.

After studying many positions concerning the right use of AI, I have reached some fundamental conclusions.

As writers, wordsmiths, and creatives in myriad disciplines, it behooves all of us to use AI for enhancement and enrichment, not for evil, and not as a replacement for our brains. That is to say, we must continue to create. We must continue to write for ourselves. Writing is a particularly vital human cognitive activity in that it gives us a vehicle to train our brains and refine our thoughts.

When we compose, we think deeply about words and semantics and forming perfect sentences to distill and communicate our thoughts. As we are thinking, we are inciting neural activity in our brains and forming new connections. This deepens our capacity to think critically and make connections across disparate disciplines leading us to *Eureka!* moments of enlightenment. As such, writing is an essential element in our struggle to become better human beings while contributing positively to the fabric of humanity.

When an AI composes a poem or writes an essay, it's simply responding to the word patterns that you entered as a prompt. The response, be it an evaluation of your writing or an intelligence report for the military, is simply a composite of the next randomly selected most-probable words that follow.

As I mentioned earlier, when you get a response from an LLM, you can hope at best for a 90% solution whereas it is more likely to be a 60% or 70% solution. No matter how much an AI is trained and fine-tuned, *humans* will always be more unpredictable and creative than LLMs.

When you use the AI as an assistant, *you* are ultimately responsible for everything that you accept from that assistant. If the AI gives you advice and you follow it, you are the one taking the risk and are responsible for the outcome. When an AI gives you a character's backstory and you adopt it, you own that backstory and any implications. If it produces content for you, it is imperative that you edit, modify, and change it thereby making it your own.

Humans must verify and oversee all content produced by AI. When you use an AI and its output, you assume complete accountability for the consequences. This is the *responsible* use of AI.

We, the public at large, have been given a tremendous gift. This technology is something very unique. After only two years, it has infiltrated many aspects of our lives from our vocabulary to how we interact with technology in general. It is a game-changer in nearly every field: educational, scientific, legal, medical, financial, recreational, etc. It is too powerful to be used carelessly. Thus, it behooves all of us to be the best we possibly can and use this technology only for the good. We are all called to protect the use of this technology and to apply it to become better people than we thought possible. As wordsmiths, we must all agree not to use AI to create harmful material, ever. This is the *right use* of AI.

When to Cite AI

The book market is currently flooded with one-week wonders wherein a human "author" creates a book largely through pasting together AI content, and then publishes it as his/her own writing. After all, AI cannot be credited as an author.[16] These human "authors" are intentionally taking advantage of the speed and fluency of the non-human producer of their material. They are committing plagiarism. This is not an ethical use of AI.

Most publishers will not handle manuscripts that are primarily AI-generated, but it is getting increasingly difficult to distinguish between AI and human composition. Therefore it is imperative that the writing community stand together and agree upon society-wide standards for the use and attribution of work that was created by AI. There is no shame in using AI as a writing assistant as long as this is properly attributed.

Give due credit to the AI model when:

- The material is substantively created using generative AI.

---

[16] March 25, 2025, "the U.S. Court of Appeals for the District of Columbia Circuit affirmed the Copyright Office's position that artificial intelligence cannot be an author under the Copyright Act." (https://www.goodwinlaw.com/en/insights/publications/2025/03/alerts-technology-dc-circuit-holds-that-ai-cannot-be-an-author)

- Plot, character development, dialogue, and other story elements were mostly developed by generative AI.
- GenAI was used extensively for research, analysis, or editing.
- A generative AI response is directly quoted.

This table shows the currently recommended citation formats.

Citation Formats for Generative AI

Citation Style	In-Text/Footnote Citation	Bibliography/End of Book Citation
MLA	(ChatGPT, response to 'How does AI generate text?', OpenAI, 1 Mar. 2025)	ChatGPT-4. OpenAI, 1 Mar. 2025, chat.openai.com.
APA	(OpenAI, 2025)	OpenAI. (2025). ChatGPT-4 (Mar. 1 version) [Large language model]. https://chat.openai.com
Chicago	1. OpenAI, ChatGPT-4, response to 'How does AI generate text?', March 1, 2025.	OpenAI. ChatGPT-4. March 1, 2025. https://chat.openai.com

For specific publications and organizations, refer to their guidelines.

By correctly attributing your use of AI, you are using AI in an *ethically transparent* manner.

Data Protection

Advocacy groups and individual creative content creators (writers, poets, musicians, artists) are in the process of legally wrangling with model developers over the protection of creators' rights. The two main points are

1) the unauthorized use of copyrighted material for *training* generative AI models, and

2) the *protection* of an individual's Intellectual Property (IP).

Using Copyrighted Works to Train

The entire available corpus of the internet was scraped to train generative AI. In other words, all textual content available on the web was used to calculate the word probabilities that are stored in the models' parameters. Furthermore, images on the web were scraped to train image generation models. It is believed that the textual and image content of the corpus includes copyrighted material. This is a serious point of contention.

Creative artists whose material was used to train the models are concerned because they weren't asked for nor did they offer consent for the use of their work to train the models. Furthermore, they were not compensated for the use of their work, and they have no guarantee that their work will not be produced as output by an LLM in the present or in the future.

With respect to the legal issue regarding consent, we have to consider the inherent nature of the internet: the web is open to scraping at anytime by anyone. Every website, social media platform, image, and blog post is subject to this wholesale automated round-up of data. In hindsight, I imagine that the developers of LLMs are chagrined that they did not make legal arrangements with major content producers such as news agencies, publishers, authors, artists, and musicians to use their data, but they did not. They are now dealing with the legal fallout. As no legal precedent for this situation exists, we await the courts' decisions.

Intellectual Property

With respect to protecting IP, since early 2023, many individuals and groups have sought to test the extent to which GenAI has the ability to regurgitate identical versions of text, lyrics, images, etc., under copyright. Throughout 2023, the LLMs were remarkably good at this. In response, additional training and fine-tuning was done and guardrails were put into place to throttle the AI's ability to produce content that resembled copyrighted material. As of the publication of this book, in most cases, it's difficult to successfully prompt a commercially-available GenAI to produce content identical or similar to copyrighted works. This is good news for all creatives.

I feel that whoever uses an LLM should bear in mind that the LLM, technically, isn't able copy anything. As I discussed in the earlier chapter, *Understanding Generative AI*, these models do not store information in their parameters. They store *probabilities* that describe how likely one word will follow another. It's that simple. If someone's work appears in an LLM's response, it is a clear indication that that work is statistically the most *likely* response to the prompt entered. In other words it appeared often enough in the training corpus that it has high probabilities of fitting a word pattern. If one wants to be generous, it's a testimony to the popularity of the work.

My recommendations to protect IP:

1) carefully manage where your IP appears,
2) refrain, at all times, from uploading and sharing sensitive, private, copyrighted, and confidential data; and,
3) ensure that all involved in marketing, endorsing, and publishing your content agree not to share your material for training purposes.

Copyright Issues

> It is well-established that copyright can protect only material that is the product of human creativity. Most fundamentally, the term "author", which is used in both the Constitution and the Copyright Act, excludes non-humans.
>
> US Copyright Office

Can you copyright the responses generated as a result of your prompts? The long-established guidance provided by the U.S. Copyright Office is that only a human-created work can be copyrighted.

The question of how to specifically treat generative AI content is addressed by guidance issued by the US Copyright Office in early 2025:

> The Office affirms that existing principles of copyright law are flexible enough to apply to this new technology, as they have applied to technological innovations in the past. It concludes that the outputs of generative AI can be protected by copyright only where a human author has determined sufficient expressive elements.

To enjoy copyright protection, LLM-generated material should reflect "expressive elements" of human input. Therefore, if you use AI as an assistant to help you create your own material, then your work should fall under copyright protection.

The guidance states: if the only human input is a prompt, then it's *excluded* from copyright protection.

> ...the outputs of generative AI can be protected by copyright only where a human author has determined sufficient expressive elements. This can include situations where a human-authored work is perceptible in an AI output, or a human makes creative arrangements or modifications of the output, **but not the mere provision of prompts.**

> Extending protection to material whose expressive elements are determined by a machine, however, would undermine rather than further the constitutional goals of copyright.

The flowchart on the next page can assist you in determining whether or not your material is protected under copyright law.

Please note: Don't list AI as a co-author!

Is Your Material Protected Under Copyright Law?

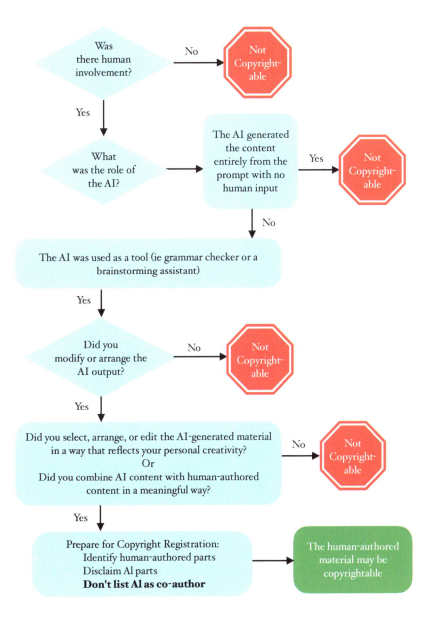

Privacy

In all communication with an LLM, it is incumbent upon you, the user, to protect both your own privacy and that of others. LLMs are products of commercial endeavors. We can assume that providers of these LLMs ultimately prioritize profit.

This means, that at all times, you should refrain from voluntarily providing the model with private and specific information about yourself or anyone else.

The private data you must guard includes:

1. Identification
    1. Name, birthdate, place of birth, mother's maiden name, addresses, phone numbers, social security numbers, and passport numbers.
2. Medical Data
    1. HIPAA information, test results, diagnoses
3. Financial Data
    1. Bank and investment account information: balances, last transaction, passwords, and account numbers.
4. Proprietary Data
    1. Business-related and product sensitive information.
5. Internet Data
    1. Usernames, account credentials, logins, pins, security questions.

Whenever I interact with an LLM, I assume that everything I type into it will be broadcast to the world. I also assume that my conversations will be used for additional training.

Most of the commercially-available LLMs have policy statements that describe how they use user input, as indicated in this table:

Current Privacy Policies for General Purpose LLM

Name	Privacy Policy
ChatGPT family chatgpt.com (Open AI)	Chats & feedback are used for training by default. Users can opt out of training via settings; Temporary chat is not stored; All chats can be deleted; Deleted chats are permanently erased after 30 days.
Claude family Claude.ai (Anthropic)	Chats are not used for training by default. Users may opt-in. Chats may be flagged for trust & safety review. Feedback may be used for training.
Gemini 2.0 ai.google (Google)	Chats are used for training by default. Users can opt-out via settings or turning off chat history. Chats stored for up to 18 months; Users can adjust this period.
LLaMA family ai.meta.com (Meta)	User's publicly shared content on Meta platforms is used for training (from 2007 to the present). In Europe and UK, users can opt-out. Users in US and Australia cannot opt-out.
Co-Pilot (Microsoft)	Chats are not used for training by default. Users can manage data preferences in settings.
Grok family x.ai (xAI)	User input, including public posts and interactions, are used for training by default. Users can opt-out via settings. All user feedback is used for training.
Perplexity perplexity.ai (Perplexity AI)	Chats are used for training by default. Users can opt-out via settings.

8 Secrets to Working with Your Assistant

LLMs are best described as probabilistic, nondeterministic machines. Instead of following rigid, rule-based logic, they generate responses by predicting and randomly choosing the most likely next word based on statistical patterns in their training data.

Because this process involves probability and randomness rather than fixed rules, the same prompt can yield different responses, making their behavior inherently nondeterministic. No one can determine what response the LLM will give.

We have learned that LLMs do more than give a "meaningful" answer to a natural language statement. LLMs are general purpose, yet powerful. They produce output across a broad spectrum of disciplines generating varied and contextually relevant outputs. They require careful guidance to produce accurate and meaningful results.

Remember the analogy about the four-year-old prodigy? Let's fast forward a few years. Think of your LLM as a very young, newly-minted assistant who is brainy but has limited experience in your field. The assistant will be enthusiastic and eager to do the job correctly. It may veer off in the wrong direction., giving you a thorough answer, but not what you intended. It may also get lazy or try to give you less than you requested. Or, maddeningly, it will make suggestions about what you want next, which throws off your chain of thought. Occasionally your assistant will blip out unexpectedly. When this happens, you gently nudge it with the prompt "Proceed."

Don't become frustrated and start insulting or speaking rudely to your assistant when it cannot do what you are asking. It'll curl up in a ball and start making yet more mistakes. It'll be almost impossible to recover and you'll have to start over with a new conversation.

If the LLM tries to give you the response you seek and it thinks it has succeeded but it has not, don't scold it. It needs training. It has an emergent capability called in-context learning. If you give it examples and feedback when it does a task correctly, then it will learn how to do that task.

Even though models can't possibly have emotions or egos, *polite words* can have a profound effect on the LLM's response. Using polite words softens your request, which changes the tone of the discourse. The responses will be clear, natural, and more professional without sounding robotic. When you use polite words, the model takes a smidgen longer to elevate the discourse and thereby add nuanced depth. Consider these two examples. First a direct request with no polite words:

> Me: Generate five character names for a historical novel set in 1920s Paris. Include gender, nationality, and a brief character note in a table.

ChatGPT: Response: Here are five character names for your 1920s Paris historical novel, complete with gender, nationality, and a brief character note:

Name	Gender	Nationality	Character Note
Henri Marchand	Male	French	A war-scarred detective investigating crimes in post-war Paris.
Claire Dubois	Female	French	A cabaret singer who dreams of becoming a silent film star.
Jakob Schneider	Male	German	A former soldier turned philosopher living in exile.
Isabella Rossi	Female	Italian	A fashion designer making waves in haute couture.
Edward Sinclair	Male	British	A foreign correspondent chronicling the pulse of a changing Europe.

Would you like additional names with specific roles or traits?

Now consider the results of the same prompt that is book-ended with polite words:

Me: Please generate five character names for a historical novel set in 1920s Paris. Could you include gender, nationality, and a brief character note in a table? Thank you!

ChatGPT: Of course! Here's a table with five character names suitable for a historical novel set in 1920s Paris:

Name	Gender	Nationality	Character Note
Élodie Moreau	Female	French	A spirited young artist navigating the bohemian circles of Montparnasse.
Thomas Whitaker	Male	British	A reserved World War I veteran and aspiring novelist drawn to Parisian cafes.
Margaux Lévesque	Female	French	A glamorous socialite with ties to avant-garde fashion and whispered scandals.

| Giovanni De Luca | Male | Italian | A charming jazz musician performing in smoky Left Bank clubs, hiding a secret past. |
| Anneliese Bauer | Female | German | A Bauhaus-trained architect struggling to make her mark in a male-dominated field. |

I asked the model for a comparison of the two lists, and asked the results to be put into a table. Here it is:

🔍 Key Observations in Table Format

Aspect	Polite Prompt (A)	Direct Prompt (B)
Tone	Warm, collaborative	Neutral, direct
Names	Slightly more poetic or elegant (e.g.,	More classic or practical (e.g.,
Chara	Emphasis on artists, socialites, and	Focus on roles tied to action,
Cultur	More texture in the descriptions	More job- or role-focused (e.g.,
Follow	Included a polite offer to expand	Brief

That being said, there *are* some tasks that yield better results with direct prompts. This includes prompts with imperative verbs, such as calculate, list, solve, extract. If you need to perform data extraction, code generation, summarization, formatting, or mathematical/logical tasks, then be direct. In most other cases, use polite language.

In all cases, the model tries to mimic you and match your style. If you greet it with "Hey!", then it will greet you with "Hey!" in return and converse in a relaxed, casual manner.

The best prompts are polite, concise, clear, and specific. As the models become increasingly adept at reasoning, they may become more successful at intuiting your intent. I believe this adage will always be true: quality in, quality out.

When you first start working with LLMs, they truly seem like magic. Please, always remember: they are simply probabilistic, nondeterministic machines. Keep repeating that to yourself as you are continually astonished at what they can do for you.

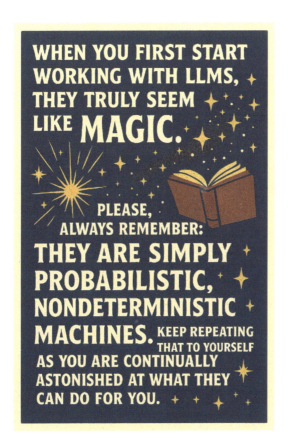

Me: Show me an interesting visualization for this text: "When you first start working with LLMs, they truly seem like magic. Please, always remember: they are simply probabilistic, nondeterministic machines. Keep repeating that to yourself as you are continually astonished at what they can do for you."

NOTES

9 Putting It All Together

Here is a simple framework of prompts to get you started with your LLM assistant. These are just a few suggestions to show you the range of conversations you might want to have with an LLM.

1. SETUP
Use Persona to establish a working environment and voice for the assistant. Provide all instructions for how you want the LLM to interact with you. Some example prompts to get you started:

> "Please act as a developmental editor who specializes in fiction and understands character-driven storytelling. You have worked on hundreds of titles and derive great satisfaction helping authors."

> (Use alternate Personas: writing assistant, writing coach, sensitivity reader, literary agent, 12-year-old target reader, etc., as appropriate.)

> "You are patient and understanding and you answer my questions with succinct answer."

> "I prefer long, in-depth answers."

> "I prefer concise, to-the-point responses."

Provide background information:

> "Here is a brief on my novel's characters and themes. Remember this as context for all future prompts."

(Paste in: character list, plot summary, setting, themes, or scene outline.)

"Here is an outline of the article that I am writing. My goal is to establish <goal of writing>."

2. Background Work
Use Flipped Interaction to help you establish key facets of your writing project. Here are some conversations you might want to start with your assistant.

"Ask questions to help me determine genre, tone, and stylistic direction for my story."

"Ask me questions to uncover the core emotional or philosophical theme of the story I want to write."

"List 5 possible story directions, and then ask which one I want to explore further."

3. Research
Use Persona to create specific experts to answer your research questions. Use Fact-Check List to identify facts that you should confirm.

Please act as an expert in <>. Cite your sources in your answers. <Ask your research question> At the end, provide a list of facts and sources.

Use Persona, Audience to conduct a mock interview with historical figures.

Act as <historical figure>. I will ask you questions about <>.
You will assume I am a <specific person or role>.

4. Opening Scene Discovery

"Ask me questions to help me determine where my story should begin and what kind of hook would be most effective."

"Help me narrow down my opening scene by asking what the reader absolutely needs to know first."

"Ask 2 questions to help determine what the reader needs to know in the first 500 words."

5. Story Development
The questions you ask the LLM about your story as it progresses will be highly individualistic. Here are some ideas:

"Pretend I am <character in the book>. <Your question to the LLM>

"Ask me three questions to help clarify this character's motivation."

"Let's brainstorm together. Please ask me questions to help me discover ways to increase tension in a story where physical danger isn't present."

"Does this character motivation make sense? Here's the setup..."

"Read this plot outline and identify possible holes or inconsistencies."

"What would a reader expect to happen next—and how can I subvert that?"

"Analyze the emotional arc of this story and suggest ways to deepen it."

"Are the stakes escalating logically throughout this summary? What's missing?"

6. Revision and Analysis

For sample prompts to help you revise and analyze your words, I refer you back to the fabulously rich examples of prompts in the section Editing, Analysis, and Feedback in Chapter 6, A Pocketful of Prompts.

In these pages, I hope you've witnessed the beginnings of a profound dialogue between writer and machine. You've seen how to begin your own conversations—how to enlist the aid of an AI assistant who, at your behest, offers information, makes suggestions, critiques, nudges, and, even surprises.

You are a writer. You will keep exploring. You will keep creating. And when you feel stuck—or need to bring forth something faster than humanly possible—remember this: *You are not alone at the page. You have an assistant who can help you.*

In the end, however,

The machine may offer words,
But it cannot write what's in
your heart.

Appendix I AI Toolkits

If you haven't already created an account with one of the commercial LLM providers, select one from the table. The models have similar capabilities; you may find the differences subtle.

You will need to create an account. You can choose various levels of use; the free level will give you access to a model for a limited number of conversations or prompts. You can't rely on a free subscription to use the LLM effectively as an assistant. It is highly recommended that you choose a model and pay a monthly fee to make full use.

The interfaces to each of the models are similar. Typically, you can enable the model to browse the internet, access uploaded documents, create and save a variety of outputs, and perform mathematical reasoning.

A conversation or chat is a series of consecutive prompts and responses. Most of the models can remember the full context of the conversation from the beginning onward, depending on the size of the context window, which is essentially the maximum number of word units (tokens) allowed per conversation. If your model stops responding after a long conversation, you may have reached a limit. Start a new conversation.

You can save, search, delete, archive, and rename conversations. You can revisit conversations and continue them. Some platforms let you organize conversations in projects.

As discussed earlier, if you are concerned about privacy and protecting your data, read each platform's privacy and data retention and training policies carefully.

As a writer, you have a dilemma: which is the best LLM to use? There is no single answer to this. However, you might want to consider building an AI Toolkit which consists of a group of LLMs for your speciality. The following table is a good starting point.

AI TOOLKITS FOR VARIOUS WRITERS

WRITER TYPE	AI TOOLKIT	WHY THESE TOOLS WORK WELL TOGETHER
Fiction Writer	Sudowrite, Claude Opus, ChatGPT; LLaMA	Sudowrite for prose & creativity; Claude for long-context editing; ChatGPT for dialogue & brainstorming; LLaMA for privacy.
Nonfiction Author	Perplexity AI, Claude Opus, ChatGPT, Zotero + AI plugin	Perplexity for fast & verifiable research; Claude for long-form structure; Opus for brainstorming & development; ChatGPT for summarization & multi-modal functionality; Zotero for source management.
Journalist	Perplexity AI Pro, Gemini, ChatGPT	Perplexity for quick fact retrieval & verification; Gemini for multi-modal input, real-time web access, & integration with Docs, Sheets, and email; ChatGPT for polishing articles & writing headlines.

Blogger & Content Creator	Jasper, Writer.com, ChatGPT, Canva (for visuals)	Jasper and Writer.com for tone and SEO; ChatGPT for variation; Canva for visual appeal.
Poet	ChatGPT, Sudowrite, Claude	ChatGPT for language play; Sudowrite for figurative language; Claude for thoughtful, theme-based editing.
Screenwriter	ChatGPT, Sudowrite, NovelAI; LLaMA 3.3	ChatGPT for brainstorming; Sudowrite for emotional arcs; NovelAI to maintain character tone; LLaMA for scene structuring.
Academic Writer	Anara.com, Perplexity Pro, Zotero, Claude, Scite.ai, NotebookLM	Anara for mindmaps, and advanced paper analysis; Perplexity + Scite for cited claims; Zotero for document control; Claude for revising dense academic prose;
Technical Writer	GitHub CoPilot, ChatGPT, Perplexity AI, NotebookLM	CoPilot for accurate documentation; ChatGPT for simplifying jargon; Perplexity for clarity; Notebook LM for document analysis and team work.
Memoirist	Claude, Sudowrite, ChatGPT (with memory)	Claude for organizing long content; Sudowrite for emotional framing; ChatGPT for remembering themes & polishing voice.
Lawyer	Harvey AI, Claude Opus, ChatGPT (GPT-4), LexisNexis AI	Harvey AI and LexisNexis for legal research accuracy and case law retrieval; Claude for complex document drafting; ChatGPT for summarizing legal arguments clearly.

C-suite Executives	Claude, ChatGPT Enterprise, Perplexity AI, Grammarly Business	Claude for strategic, long-form business narratives; ChatGPT for concise summaries & executive coordination; Perplexity for market & competitive research; Grammarly Business for polish.
Military Action Officer	ChatGPT Enterprise, Claude Opus, Perplexity AI, Palantir AI	ChatGPT for rapid briefing preparation; Claude for detailed operational reports; Perplexity for intelligence verification; Palantir for integrating multi-source intelligence effectively.
Data-Driven Storyteller	NotebookLM, ChatGPT, Observable	NotebookLM for data synthesis; Observable for publishing interactive narratives; ChatGPT for narrative structuring and clarity.

Good luck and may you prompt with aplomb!

Appendix II Glossary

Agentic AI

AI systems designed to take autonomous actions toward achieving a goal, often across multiple steps and decisions without constant user input.

Artificial Intelligence (AI)

The broad field of systems that can do tasks that typically require human intelligence, such as learning, reasoning, or problem-solving.

Augmented Prompting

Enhancing a prompt by including additional input that may include uploading a document, image, or data; inserting reference text; or supplying structured background material to guide the AI more effectively.

Audience-Performer (prompt pattern)

A pattern whereby the model is instructed that the user is a particular character or personality and tailors responses.

Bias (in AI systems)

The tendency of AI to produce skewed or unfair results due to limitations or imbalances in the training data.

Context Window

The amount of text (measured in tokens) an AI model can "remember" and use to generate a response. Longer context windows allow for more detailed inputs and continuity.

Disallowed Outputs

Categories of responses the AI is restricted from producing. Understanding these helps avoid frustration when the model refuses certain tasks or topics.

Emergent Capabilities

Unexpected abilities that arise in larger models that were neither explicitly programmed nor present in smaller versions.

Fact-Checklist (prompt pattern)

A pattern where you ask the AI to provide a list of key facts in the response generated; allowing the user to review for accuracy.

Fine-tuning

Further training a pre-trained AI model on specific data to specialize its behavior, style, or knowledge for particular tasks or domains.

Flipped Interaction (prompt pattern)

A pattern where the user asks the model to ask questions to the user to gather information from the user.

Game Play (prompt pattern)

A pattern in which the user invites AI to play an interactive game together. This is useful for interactive quizzes, what-if scenario planning, designing mystery games, interactive story-telling and so on.

Generative AI

A subfield of natural language processing in which new content such as stories, poems, images, or code based on patterns learned from training data is generated.

Guardrails

Built-in rules or restrictions that help AI generate safe, ethical, and appropriate responses.

Hallucination

When an AI generates information that sounds plausible but is factually incorrect or entirely invented.

Intellectual Property

Legal rights that protect original creations, such as books or artwork. AI-generated content raises important questions around authorship and ownership.

Iterative Prompting

The process of refining prompts in steps, using the AI's previous output as a foundation to improve or expand results—much like revising a draft.

Large Language Model (LLM)

An AI trained on massive text datasets to understand and generate language. Examples include GPT-4, Claude, and Gemini.

Machine Learning

The method by which computers learn from data to improve performance, often without explicit programming for each task.

Multimodal AI

AI that can process and respond to more than one type of input or output including text, images, and sound, allowing for richer interactions.

Neural Networks

The layered structures that form the "brain" of AI systems, allowing them to learn patterns from data by simulating interconnected neurons.

Non-deterministic

Describes how AI responses may vary even when given the same prompt multiple times, adding randomness and reducing predictability.

Parameters

The internal settings (often in the billions) that determine how an AI model processes information and produces responses.

Persona (prompt pattern)

A pattern whereby the AI is asked to assume a specific role, character, or voice—like a tutor, detective, or historical figure— tailoring the tone and content accordingly.

Prompt Chaining

Linking multiple prompts in sequence so that each builds on the previous one—helpful for planning novels, editing drafts, or building layered characters.

Prompt Engineering

The practice of designing prompts strategically to guide AI output. A critical skill for writers who want consistent, high-quality responses.

Reflection (prompt pattern)

A pattern whereby the AI is asked to evaluate its own output—checking clarity, accuracy, tone, or creativity. Encourages refinement and more thoughtful results.

Retrieval-Augmented Generation (RAG)

A method where the AI searches and retrieves relevant information from outside sources (e.g., documents, knowledge bases) before generating a response.

Token

A unit of text (such as a word or part of a word) used in processing. The number of tokens limits how much the AI can consider at one time.

Training

The phase where an AI model learns from large text datasets, developing an understanding of language, facts, and writing styles.

Transfer Learning

A technique in machine learning where a model trained on one task is adapted to perform a new, related task. Instead of starting from scratch, the model "transfers" the knowledge it already has such as understanding grammar, tone, or structure, to help with a new application.

Transformer
A foundational AI architecture that allows models to analyze relationships between all parts of a sentence or document, enabling nuanced and cohesive language generation.

Appendix III Media One-Sheet

MEDIA ONE-SHEET

Conversing with AI: A Handbook for Writers
by ML Brei

ABOUT THE BOOK

Conversing with AI is a practical guide to mastering communication with large language models (LLMs). Based on over two years of research and experimentation, this book distills the best of academic insights and hands-on experience into usable techniques for writers working with AI.

With real-world examples and accessible pattern frameworks—including those developed by Dr. Jules White's lab at Vanderbilt University—this book empowers readers to harness the full potential of AI through structured, repeatable prompting methods.

ABOUT THE AUTHOR

ML Brei is a researcher, author, and educator in the field of generative AI. Fascinated by the release of the first public LLM, she immersed herself into study and experimentation, building expertise that led to the creation of *Conversing with AI*. Her work bridges academic theory and practical application, making the tools of AI more approachable for writers,, creatives, professionals, educators and everyday users.

KEY TOPICS & THEMES

• Using structured prompt patterns to outperform trial-and-error

• Using LLMs as collaborators, coaches, and rehearsal partners

• Lessons from AI research and how they translate into practice

- Ethical use of AI and correct attribution

IDEAL AUDIENCE

Authors, educators, students, lawyers, journalists, and anyone looking to understand how to effectively work with generative AI tools.

MEDIA HOOKS

- "I trained an AI to interview me—and it worked."

- "The secret to great AI output isn't the AI—it's the prompt."

INTERVIEW QUESTIONS (Suggested for Media)

- What inspired you to write *Conversing with AI*?

- Can anyone learn to work with AI tools, or is it just for techies?

- What are a few patterns from the book that listeners could try today?

- How has your approach to work changed since integrating LLMs?

- What do you see as the future of prompt engineering?

CONTACT

Website: meripointbooks.com

References

Alexander, Christopher, Sara Ishikawa, and Murray Silverstein. *A Pattern Language: Towns, Buildings, Construction*. New York: Oxford University Press, 1977.

Hooper, Theresa V. Echoes of the Hurrians: Tracing an Ancient People from the Caucasus Mountains to Celt-Iberia to the Spanish New World. 2nd ed. Meripoint Books, 2025.

Mollick, Ethan. Co-Intelligence: Living and Working with AI. New York: Portfolio, 2024.

Mols, Roger. "Histoire de la crèche de Noël d'après un ouvrage récent." *Nouvelle Revue Théologique* 81, no. 10 (1959): 1049–1072.

Wolfram, Stephen. What Is ChatGPT Doing ... and Why Does It Work? Champaign, IL: Wolfram Media, 2023.

The following papers and studies can be found on the internet.

Doshi, Anil R., and Oliver P. Hauser. "Generative AI Enhances Individual Creativity but Reduces the Collective Diversity of Novel Content." *Science Advances* 10, no. 28 (July 12, 2024): eadn5290. https://doi.org/10.1126/sciadv.adn5290.

Ren, Hui, Joanna Materzyńska, Rohit Gandikota, David Bau, Antonio Torralba, et al. "Art-Free Generative Models: Art Creation Without Graphic Art Knowledge." arXiv preprint arXiv:2412.00176 (2024).

Schulhoff, Sander, Michael Ilie, Nishant Balepur, Konstantine Kahadze, Amanda Liu, Chenglei Si, and Yinheng Li, *et al.* "The Prompt Report: A Systematic Survey of Prompting Techniques." arXiv preprint arXiv:2406.06608 (2024).

Sikander, Binyamin, Jason J. Baker, Can D. Deveci, Lars Lund, and Jacob Rosenberg. "ChatGPT-4 and Human Researchers Are Equal in Writing Scientific Introduction Sections: A Blinded, Randomized, Non-inferiority Controlled Study." *Cureus* 15, no. 11 (November 2023): e49019. https://doi.org/10.7759/cureus.49019

Verma, Sahil, Royi Rassin, Arnav Das, Gantavya Bhatt, Preethi Seshadri, Chirag Shah, and Jeff Bilmes, et al. "How Many Van Goghs Does It Take to Van Gogh? Finding the Imitation Threshold." arXiv preprint arXiv:2410.15002 (2024).

Wei, Jason, Yi Tay, Rishi Bommasani, Colin Raffel, Barret Zoph, Sebastian Borgeaud, and Dani Yogatama, et al. "Emergent Abilities of Large Language Models." *Transactions on Machine Learning Research* (2022).

White, J., Fu, Q., Hays, S., Sandborn, M., Olea, C., Gilbert, H., Elnashar, A., Spencer-Smith, J., & Schmidt, D. C. (2023). A prompt pattern catalog to enhance prompt engineering with ChatGPT [White paper]. arXiv. https://arxiv.org/abs/2302.11382

For more information on prompt patterns see: https://www.vanderbilt.edu/generative-ai/prompt-patterns/

Artificial Intelligence Assistance

Select passages and images in this book feature responses generated by ChatGPT, a large language model created by OpenAI. These interactions were part of a creative and exploratory process, guided by custom prompts written by the author.

OpenAI. ChatGPT (March 2025 version). https://chat.openai.com/

*A*bout the Author

ML Brei is an author, educator, and prompt engineering consultant with a passion for empowering others at the intersection of language and technology. A graduate of Smith College and a member of its inaugural Computer Science class, ML Brei brings over 19 years of experience in teaching, curriculum development, and publishing to her work.

She is the founder of Meripoint Books LLC, an independent press dedicated to thoughtful, purpose-driven literature. Her diverse portfolio includes fiction, nonfiction, and educational materials, with titles such as *A Different Type of Soul* (2022) and *The Christian Symbols of the Twelve Days of Christmas* (2022). Known for her practical wisdom and visionary insight, ML Brei now helps writers, military personnel, and educators harness the power of AI through structured prompting and ethical guidance.

meripointbooks.com

*T*reat your LLM well and you will be well-rewarded.

www.ingramcontent.com/pod-product-compliance
Lightning Source LLC
LaVergne TN
LVHW012316070326
832902LV00004BA/76